GOD'S SURPRISES *for the* CHRISTMAS SEASON

God's Surprises for the Christmas Season
Blessings and Broken Plans

God's Surprises for the Christmas Season
978-1-7910-4213-4
978-1-7910-4214-1 eBook

God's Surprises for the Christmas Season DVD
978-1-7910-4217-2

Also by Susan Robb

Remember: God's Covenants and the Cross

The Angels of Christmas: Hearing God's Voice in Advent

Seven Words: Listening to Christ from the Cross

Called: Hearing and Responding to God's Voice

On Purpose: Finding God's Voice in Your Passion
(with Magrey deVega, Sam McGlothlin,
and Jevon Caldwell-Gross)

Cover description: Features a peaceful snow-covered village beneath a warm golden sky with gently falling snow. Evergreen trees, including a decorated Christmas tree, surround homes and a church with glowing windows, creating a welcoming holiday scene. Centered above the village, the title, *God's Surprises for the Christmas Season*, appears in large burgundy serif letters with decorative gold flourishes. A burgundy banner below contains the subtitle, *Blessings and Broken Plans*. The author's name, Susan Robb, is displayed in gold lettering within a decorative plaque on a dark green argyle-patterned background at the bottom of the cover.

GOD'S SURPRISES *for the* CHRISTMAS SEASON

BLESSINGS AND BROKEN PLANS

SUSAN ROBB

ABINGDON PRESS | NASHVILLE

God's Surprises for the Christmas Season
Blessings and Broken Plans

Library of Congress Control Number: 2026942500
978-1-7910-4213-4

MANUFACTURED IN THE UNITED STATES OF AMERICA

CONTENTS

WATCH YOUR STUDY ANYTIME, ANYWHERE.

Access your *God's Surprises for the Christmas Season* videos and leader resources on any device with your Amplify Media account.

GET STARTED IN TWO STEPS

1 Scan the QR code or go to My.AmplifyMedia.com /amplify/redeem

2 Create your free account and enter your companion code

Companion Code
SRANNS3H

Once You're In

- Videos and leader resources saved to your account
- Watch anytime on phone, tablet, or TV
- Come back anytime at My.AmplifyMedia.com

Keep Track of Your Log In Info

Email ______________________________

Password ___________________________

Companion code subject to expiration. Code may be redeemed only by the recipient of this book. Code may not be transferred or sold separately. Internet connection required.

AMPLIFY™ MEDIA

PREFACE

It's late September 2025 in Dallas. Fall has officially begun, but the temperatures outside are still commensurate with our wilting summers. To be sure, the thought of drinking a hot pumpkin spiced latte is far from most of our minds while we wait and hope for cooler temperatures indicative of fall. Although it doesn't feel like Advent outside, I've begun writing this book, thinking about all the stories and themes that go with the church's preparation for Christmas.

I find, when I'm working on a book, that writing in Bridwell Library, part of Perkins School of Theology at Southern Methodist University, keeps me focused and away from the many distractions that beckon me to leave my writing desk in my home. To me, writing at Bridwell has become a spiritual practice. For my habit, as I am walking across campus to the library, is to first duck inside the chapel, just adjacent to the library, to pray and ask for God's guidance and direction as I write. It was in this chapel that I first worshipped with professors and fellow seminarians after answering God's surprising call to attend seminary twenty-five years ago. This space is full of precious memories for me. It is holy ground. So much so, that I sometimes wonder if I should remove my shoes before entering, like God tells Moses to do in Exodus 3:5.

This week in Dallas has been a difficult one. I am part of an interfaith clergy group that holds prayer vigils outside of Dallas

ICE headquarters every Monday morning. With the climate of vitriol, violence, and fear that is in our country today regarding immigration, we choose to be a praying presence. We pray for those migrants who are coming for their regular check-in interviews, for those who are being detained, for those who are afraid of what might happen to them when they go inside: Will they be detained? Deported? Will they have to leave their children and families behind, even as they are following the requirements of the law? We pray for the ICE agents and staff who work there, that, in the stress of their jobs, they might treat each person they encounter with the dignity and compassion that should be afforded every child of God, regardless of status. And we pray for everyone's safety. We also hold signs in Spanish and English reminding all who enter (migrants and staff alike) that we are praying for them, that they are loved, that all are neighbors, and that *all* are constitutionally entitled to due process.

A week ago today our group held vigil. Two days later, a lone gunman targeted the headquarters, killing two detainees and critically injuring another in the space with which we are so familiar. We are devastated, and our city and our nation are currently in turmoil over this situation. And so, when I came to the library to write today, I wasn't quite sure how to make the emotional, spiritual, or creative leap from a hot, fearful, tumultuous fall day in Dallas, to the hope, peace, love, and joy promised in the season of Advent. I couldn't wait to get to the chapel, because I desperately needed to be *in* the chapel—a space where I, like Moses at Mount Sinai (who goes up the mountain about eight times!), have met God over and over again.

Just stepping across the threshold of Perkins Chapel began to bring peace to my soul. As I peered through the narthex windows into the chapel, I could see someone seated at the organ console on the chancel, presumably a music student there for organ practice, so I remained seated on a bench in the narthex and began to pray, "Lord, you know what a dark time it has been in our city, in our world, and in so many of our souls. Please offer your Spirit and guidance today to help me shift my attention from all of the violence, hatred, and confusion that surrounds us in this moment, to the message of Advent and the Christmas season." As I continued to pray, God, through the organist, offered a great surprise! In the middle of this unseasonably hot fall day, the organ burst forth with bold grandeur, and the chapel literally vibrated with the tune "Come, Thou Long Expected Jesus," one of the leading hymns of the Advent season (and one of my favorites).

As the hymn continued, I smiled and gave thanks to God for this unexpected confirmation of what the Advent season is about, especially on this day. The opening verse of the hymn begins:

> Come, thou long expected Jesus, born to set thy people free;
>
> From our fears and sins release us, let us find our rest in thee.[1]

The hymn reminded me of the world into which Jesus was born: a world full of fear and darkness; of violence, injustice, and oppression; of political and sometimes religious unrest. A world full of the broken dreams and broken plans of God's people. A world, in some respects, not so different from our own. And into this world, then and now, God sends us light, hope, peace, love, and joy through the surprising gift of the birth of a baby. God's own self incarnate.

I walked into the chapel today with a heavy heart, grieving for two families who unnecessarily and tragically lost husbands, fathers, and sons due to unhinged political violence. Families whose dreams and plans for their futures have been shattered. I entered feeling impotent to change a culture that continues to foment division and hatred toward the "other." Yet, in that sacred space, I met, and was surprised by, once again, the God of the universe, who came to us in the form of a vulnerable and helpless child to offer us God's own radical, powerful, and infinite supply of love, peace, joy, and hope. I left the chapel bathed in Advent light that shines in the world's darkness, assured that the Christ who came to us and was born to us so many years ago continues to come into our broken paths and plans to surprise us with his love and new plans for a future full of hope.

Throughout this book, I hope that you will delight in the surprises that God offers to each of the biblical characters in the Gospels' Nativity stories, as each person encounters the blessings of their own broken plans. And may you also find God's surprises and blessings in your own life as you journey through this Advent season.

Susan Robb
September 29, 2025

INTRODUCTION

God's Surprises for the Christmas Season

I don't know about you, but as the Advent season approaches, I get more and more excited. One would think that having grown up in the church and having served in church ministry for so many years, heading into another Advent season might seem old hat or make one feel blasé. But that's not the case for me! I'm excited to begin singing Advent hymns and Christmas carols in church, and to the chagrin of my family, in my car and home as well (I'm not exactly known for having a beautiful singing voice). I get absolutely giddy just thinking about singing "O Come, O Come, Emmanuel" the first Sunday in Advent and wish we could keep it on a regular rotation year-round as part of our order of worship.

I'm excited to follow the news of the birth of not just one, but two babies, John the Baptist as well as Jesus of Nazareth. Anticipating hearing Mary's story once again, of saying yes to God's plan for the future of the world, and her role in it, fills me with awe and hope. And don't all of us have a sympathetic heart for Joseph as he contemplates what decision he should make regarding his intended bride when he discovers she is pregnant and he is not the father? Every year, don't we wait with bated breath, are surprised yet again, and then rejoice when Joseph decides to believe the angel's news, keep his vow to be Mary's husband, and accept his new role as earthly father to our Savior? We eagerly follow the gift-laden wise men (also known as magi) and their guiding star, from the east to Jerusalem and finally on to Bethlehem, hoping when they encounter the hard-hearted King Herod in Jerusalem that this year's journey for them will be different. We hope that the Christ Child's life, and the lives of Bethlehem's children, will not be endangered because of the magi's appearance before the power-hungry Herod; and that the magi will not be forced to take a different and clandestine route home in order to protect the life of the divine child once they find him and bow down to pay him homage. I'm thrilled once again, and I'm guessing you are as well, when the dark night sky over the unsuspecting shepherds' heads is suddenly filled with the glorious light and voices of angels announcing the birth of the One the world had been waiting for for centuries.

We've heard the stories over and over again but still find such joy, surprise, and wonder around every corner in their retelling. In the midst of recounting them, we also discover hope for our world and our lives once again, no matter how much darkness surrounds us. We wait with anticipation to hear the good news Christ's birth brings for all people—yes, *all* people. Every year, we want to experience this old news in a new way. Just like when we find a new nugget of truth in a more than familiar Scripture reading, we want to find wisdom that speaks into our lives today as we hear these familiar stories of our faith heritage. The reason we can experience these stories in surprising, new, and redemptive ways is because our lives and the circumstances of our world are different each year.

The year I was pregnant with our first child, I felt a close affinity to Mary (as most women who are pregnant during the Christmas season do) as we awaited the birth of the child we desperately desired. The wonder of my husband and me being cocreators with God in bringing new life into the world was indescribable. Years later, I felt more like Joseph, as my daughter had a frightening medical emergency during the Christmas season. Joseph's story of trust in God, and his sober and protective action, gave me the courage and faith I needed during that time to be an advocate for my own child. His story also filled me with peace during a frightening time. The glorious surprise of growing new life and the surprise of sensing God's peace and protection in the midst of uncertainty were both blessings offered through the remembrance of these old but living stories.

I don't know the circumstances in your life this season—if you will be surrounded by the joy of exciting circumstances, or if you will be facing anxious or lonely moments or ones filled with grief. But the good news of these ancient stories is that no matter the circumstances in our life or in our world, they always bring good news and a hope for the future, even when things look bleak. If you have much to celebrate this year, may you share your joy with others and reach out to those for whom this season may not be "the most wonderful time of the year." And if you are facing troubled times this year, my prayer for you is that you will find God's surprises when and where you least expect them, along with the blessings that flow from those surprises. Maybe you will be surprised by the quiet and reassuring knowledge that God is with you, even in a dark hour. Maybe your surprise will come in an unbidden deep sense of God's all-encompassing love for you that will lead you to experience peace and joy in the midst of a troubling time. Whatever your circumstances, may these old stories bring you new surprises and blessings this season.

What we may not have considered as we listened to these stories in the past—of Mary's encounter with Gabriel, Joseph's dreams, the magi's long journey, or the shepherd's surprising visit and birth announcement by the heavenly host—is that each of these biblical characters had no conception of what was about to unfold in their lives. They were going about their everyday existence, making plans that had little to do with ushering in the kingdom of God. They were planning a wedding, building a new home for a bride, gazing at and studying the stars, and tending flocks by night. But God had something new and exciting in store for them and the world. Their immediate plans were suddenly and surprisingly interrupted, broken by the God of the universe. Those interruptions came unbidden, unasked for. Some were unwelcome at first, but all of these interruptions, changes, and detours that resulted in broken plans and paths also opened up space for incredible surprises and blessings for all involved. Indeed, they opened space for the blessing of the entire world.

Advent, from the Latin *adventus,* or "coming," is a time of preparation for the coming of the Messiah, of his coming again into our hearts and lives this season and for his return one day. It's a time of waiting and watching, a time of making room for the newborn Savior in our busy and hectic lives. It's a time of celebrating miraculous pregnancies and the birth of new life in, for, and among us. It's also a time to reflect on the fact that Jesus's birth brought disruption, interruption, changing of plans, detours, and disappointments. But out of those disruptions, disappointments, and detours came trust, joy, and blessing. This can be true in our lives today as well.

Haven't we all experienced unwanted or unexpected interruptions in our lives that led us down a different path than we imagined? It often happens that even what seems at the time to be an unwelcome detour or roadblock turns out to be a blessing. A job that you didn't get or a relationship that suddenly ended can open up new, joyful possibilities, sometimes even a new calling. In our disappointment, we might have felt as if we were the only ones going through such an event, but Advent teaches us that this is universal to the human experience. It's often just how God works in our lives.

The goal of this book is to help you better understand the effect of the interruptions facing the biblical characters involved in the birth narratives of Jesus, appreciate the connections to the stories and prophetic voices of the Hebrew Scriptures, and see how all of this relates to you, your community, the church, and the world around us.

As we engage in these stories of Advent, we all will be confronted by the voice of the angel asking us to say yes to God's desire to use us as wombs in which to allow the Christ Child to be born in us this season. We will be confronted by the kind of dilemma Joseph faces when he is met with the unexpected and inexplicable, and we, too, will be asked to trust God as we face our fears and exhibit our faith and trust through action. We will be encouraged by the relentless determination of the magi to find, pay homage to, and protect the Christ Child, and by our call to do the same. Finally, we will be confronted by the awe of the shepherds as they witness the angelic chorus in the night sky and as they embrace their new role in sharing the good news of the birth of Christ to everyone they encounter—a role God asks us to take on as well.

As you watch the lives of these characters being interrupted by the God of the universe, calling them to a different and sometimes difficult path, so too will your life be surprisingly interrupted and your journey set on a new path and call. This is a call that can bring good news of great joy to a world in need of light, life, hope, and peace; a call that will bring blessing to your broken plans and to those you encounter as you travel your new path.

May this Advent study be a blessing to you and to all you encounter this season and in years to come.

MARY

The Surprise of Calling

CHAPTER 1

CHAPTER 1

Mary

The Surprise of Calling

In the sixth month the angel Gabriel was sent by God to a town in Galilee called Nazareth, to a virgin engaged to a man whose name was Joseph, of the house of David. The virgin's name was Mary. And he came to her and said, "Greetings, favored one! The Lord is with you." But she was much perplexed by his words and pondered what sort of greeting this might be. The angel said to her, "Do not be afraid, Mary, for you have found favor with God. And now, you will conceive in your womb and bear a son, and you will name him Jesus. He will be great and will be called the Son of the Most High, and the Lord God will give to him the throne of his ancestor David. He will reign over the house of Jacob forever, and of his kingdom there will be no end."

(Luke 1:26-33)

O that you would tear open the heavens and come down,
so that the mountains would quake at your presence...
so that the nations might tremble at your presence!
When you did awesome deeds that we did not expect,
you came down; the mountains quaked at your presence.
From ages past no one has heard,
no ear has perceived,

no eye has seen any God besides you,
who works for those who wait for him.
(Isaiah 64:1, 2b-4)

For the most part, young women today have dreams of what their weddings might be like long before a groom enters the picture. Church or destination wedding? What kind of dress, flowers, cake? How many bridesmaids and the color of their dresses? What kind of reception given their or their parents' means? Band or DJ? Fellowship hall of the church or a grand venue?

Long before I met my husband, visions of what kind of wedding I might have danced in my head. It would *definitely* be a church wedding, with all of my and my very large family's friends (and his). A few close friends and family would serve as bridesmaids, and dancing would be requisite at the reception. These plans would probably take six to nine months to implement, with engagement parties and wedding showers scattered in between.

My husband and I, already not particularly young sweethearts, dated for two years. We were well matched in values and what we wanted in a relationship and marriage, but in our discussions around what a wedding might look like, we were polar opposites. He preferred to elope (my, as I called it, "big, fat, Scotch-Irish/English family," consisting of close to a hundred, was a bit overwhelming to someone whose entire extended family could fit around one large dining table), and well, you can see how that differed from my own vision.

When the big evening came, and Ike proposed, I was over the moon (as was he)! What surprised me, after the thrill of a ring box appearing from his pocket, and the question, "Will you marry me?" followed by my enthusiastic "Yes!" was that next, immediately out of his mouth came the words, "How fast can you pull this thing off?" And without thinking, I responded, "Six weeks!"

I'm not sure what I was thinking, but the wedding we wound up with was one neither of us expected or envisioned. We were each sent on a detour of sorts from our original hopes and dreams, but one in the end that led us not to my wedding or his but to one that was uniquely *ours.* With the help of my mother-in-law-to-be, who lived nearby, within three days I had the wedding and reception venues booked, minister confirmed, and wedding cake and invitations ordered. I bought a beautiful wedding dress off the rack and had it altered to fit. We each had one attendant, and mine chose her own dress. We married in a beautiful chapel at the church I attended instead of its expansive sanctuary, with seventy-five of our truly closest family and friends. It was a wedding that focused more on our future marriage and how we would live our life together than the trappings of a big, expensive wedding. In the end, it was perfect for us and brought us both great joy.

What we had each dreamed of separately didn't come to fruition, but the broken plans we experienced were truly a blessing. The memory of our wedding day is still one of our greatest joys.

Mary's Broken Plans

Mary of Nazareth didn't have the wedding she had hoped and planned for either. In Jesus's day, weddings had many of the same components ours do today. There is an engagement, also called a betrothal, a covenant made before God, prayers and blessings pronounced, and an elaborate celebration afterward. The engagement in the time of Jesus was actually contractual. The couple could be betrothed from the time they were younger, or later as the bride approached the physical capability to bear children. Typically, the couple's parents arranged the marriages, but some sprang from mutual attractions. However, once the couple was engaged, it was legally binding. Even though the marriage would not be consummated until a later date, if one party decided to call off the wedding, a divorce decree would be required. So, from the time of the engagement, the couple was entering into a covenant relationship in which God was witness to their obligations to each other.

In preparation for the couple living together, the bridegroom would spend time at his parents' house building a new home, or room, for the couple to live in. There is no firm indication in the Bible that there was a religious ceremony like we have today on one's wedding day, for the covenant had already been made. But what is certain is that the nuptial celebrations consisted of a procession from the home of the bride to the bridegroom's house (Matthew 25:6), and both the bride and the bridegroom would have been beautifully adorned (Psalm 45:14-15; Isaiah 49:18; Jeremiah 2:32).

The wedding procession would begin with the bridegroom and his friends arriving at the bride's home, often at night (remember the parable of the bridesmaids who had to keep their lamps lit and stay awake while waiting for the bridegroom in Matthew 25:1-9). The groom and his companions would then escort the bride and her bridesmaids to his parents' home and the home that he had prepared for them. Along the way, the procession would begin to burgeon, with friends and family members joining them as they festively processed through the village. It is believed that once the couple arrived at the groom's parents' home, the parents would offer a blessing of the marriage, and the bride and her maids would retreat to a room set aside for them. The next day, a weeklong wedding feast would begin that included food, music, dancing, and games. The feast came to a conclusion when the bride moved into the groom's home, where they would begin their new life together.

My guess is that Mary would have been anticipating and preparing for the day of her and Joseph's wedding feast for some time. While she worked on her adornments for that day, and he built their new home, Mary no doubt anticipated with excitement what it would be like when Joseph and his friends appeared at her parents' house to lead her to *their* new home.

And in the midst of Mary's best-laid plans, God broke into her life through the angel Gabriel with an unexpected and surprising announcement, sending all of her plans for a beautiful wedding feast, and an unassuming life with her husband in the little village of Nazareth, in a direction no one could have anticipated—least of all her.

And then: "Greetings, favored one! The Lord is with you" (Luke 1:28). Out of nowhere it seems, the angel Gabriel appears before Mary. The Bible doesn't tell us where Mary was when Gabriel addressed her, so art throughout the ages has depicted the angel appearing to Mary in various ways and places. Some paintings show Gabriel appearing in Mary's room as she's sitting on her bed, others as she's kneeling in prayer, and some outside her home. Some show Gabriel to have wings as he hovers near her making his announcement, while one image simply imagines his presence as a bright light. No matter how or where Gabriel made his presence known to Mary, it must have been shocking, and probably more than a little frightening. That's why his next words to Mary are what most angels' opening statement is to the subject they are visiting: "Do not be afraid."

> *Do not be afraid, Mary, for you have found favor with God. And now, you will conceive in your womb and bear a son, and you will name him Jesus. He will be great and will be called the Son of the Most High, and the Lord God will give to him the throne of his ancestor David. He will reign over the house of Jacob forever, and of his kingdom there will be no end.*
>
> *(Luke 1:30-33)*

If you have grown up in the church, or simply seen a few Christmas pageants, Gabriel's words are probably not surprising to you. But imagine if you lived in the first century and were listening to this story for the first time. This news would no doubt sound totally unbelievable and shocking—unless you had heard or read the first twenty-five verses of Luke's Gospel that prepare us, and the readers of old, for Mary's story.

In those verses, we learn that the angel Gabriel was quite busy prior to his visit to Mary. Six months before, he appeared to a priest named Zechariah, who is married to a woman named Elizabeth. They are childless because Elizabeth is "barren," unable to conceive, and they both "were getting on in years" (Luke 1:7).

If you had been a Jewish person living in those times, your ears would already be tingling, and you could almost bet you knew what would happen next! Excitement would mount, for if an angel visits a childless couple, there's bound to be a miraculous pregnancy and the birth of a son who will play an important role in God's plans for the world.

The Hebrew Scriptures, or Old Testament, are replete with stories of infertile women (old and young) becoming pregnant at God's intervention. And their sons do not grow up to be ordinary people. Abraham and Sarah are one hundred years old and ninety-nine years old, respectively, when their son, Isaac, is born, who becomes the fulfillment of God's covenant with Abraham that he will be the father of multitudes and nations, that he will be blessed by God to be a blessing to all the nations (Genesis 12:1-4). Other famous once-infertile women and their sons include Rebekah, the mother of Jacob and Esau (Jacob had twelve sons, whose descendants became the twelve tribes of Israel); Rachel, the mother of Joseph, who saved his family from famine and led them to Egypt; the unnamed mother of Samson; and Hannah, who gave birth to the great judge, priest, and prophet Samuel.

And now Elizabeth and her husband, Zechariah, in their old age, will be blessed with a son named John, or as we know him, John the Baptist, who will prepare the hearts and minds of a waiting Israel for the coming Messiah.

One of the purposes the author of Luke has in telling Elizabeth's story is to recall the Old Testament stories of God blessing people with miraculous pregnancies, so that we are prepared when we hear Mary's story of God blessing a young peasant virgin with a miraculous pregnancy. While the world was waiting and praying for a savior, he would arrive in a most unconventional and miraculous way.

So let's get back to Gabriel and Mary. It is the sixth month of Elizabeth's pregnancy when Gabriel brings his extraordinary news to Mary (Luke 1:26). Gabriel drops a barrage of surprising information on Mary all at once: She is not only favored, but the reason she is favored is that God has chosen her to conceive and bear a son, who will be named Jesus (meaning "he saves"). This child will be "great" and will be called the "Son of the Most High," and he will be given the throne of David by God (1:32), where there will be no end to his kingdom. "He will reign over the house of Jacob forever" (1:33).

A lot must have been swirling through Mary's mind. Israel had not had a Davidic king for over four centuries, since the Babylonian Empire sacked Jerusalem and sent most of its people into exile. Many were hoping that God's promise to King David, Israel's greatest king, made almost a thousand years before would come true: that David's kingdom would last *forever* (2 Samuel 7:16). The hope was that someone from David's lineage would rise up and save them from their oppression by the Roman Empire, that a military and political leader like David would once again rule Israel. That is why before Gabriel speaks, Luke tells us that Mary's intended husband, Joseph, is "of the house of David" (Luke 1:27), which Mary would have already known.

Then Gabriel speaks, telling Mary that she will have a son, Jesus, the Son of God and heir to David's throne. Swirling through her mind might have been questions like, *Will this child be born to*

Joseph and me after our wedding feast? But when is this conception going to take place if the wedding is still some time off? Mary must have also felt favored, honored, and humbled that of all of the young women in Judah, she, a lowly peasant girl from a small village, would be chosen by God to be the mother of the great Davidic king that her world had been waiting for for centuries.

So Mary asks, "How can this be, since I am a virgin?" (Luke 1:34). And Gabriel astounds Mary with his answer: "The Holy Spirit will come upon you, and the power of the Most High will overshadow you; therefore the child to be born will be holy; he will be called the Son of God" (v. 35). This conception will be no ordinary one. Although kings were sometimes referred to as God's sons in the Hebrew Scriptures because of their divinely appointed relationship with God, this child will truly be *the* Son of God.

Gabriel must have known that Mary was still trying to comprehend the barrage of information laid upon her when he adds another bit of current news that takes her back to God's miraculous intervention in bringing about the birth of important ancestors in Israel's past. Gabriel shares that Mary's relative Elizabeth, who was known to be infertile, and is past her reproductive years, has conceived a son. She is now six months pregnant. "For nothing will be impossible with God" (Luke 1:37).

"Nothing will be impossible with God." These words recall God's rhetorical question to Abraham as God announces that Abraham and his extremely old and childless wife, Sarah, are about to conceive a child that will usher in God's covenant with Abraham. "Is anything too wonderful for the LORD?" (Genesis 18:14).

And now Elizabeth, Mary's relative who had been unable to have children, has been given the ability to conceive a son, John, who will someday prepare the hearts of the people of Israel to receive their new Messiah and king, Mary's son, Jesus. God's covenant made through Abraham, Isaac, and Jacob will now be extended and fulfilled through her own miraculously conceived son.

Mary, no doubt, is weighing how she is going to tell Joseph what has happened and wondering if he will be willing to believe her outrageous-sounding story. There will be whispers and gossip about her condition when it becomes evident to others. There will be no wedding of her dreams, then. But she is favored by God, and God has offered her the call and opportunity of a lifetime, to be the mother of the Son of David, the Son of God. If she accepts God's change of plans and God's new call on her life, the prayers of the people since the days of Isaiah and the Babylonian exile will be answered through her:

O that you would tear open the heavens and come down,
so that the mountains would quake at your presence…
so that the nations might tremble at your presence!
When you did awesome deeds that we did not expect,
you came down; the mountains quaked at your presence.
From ages past no one has heard,
no ear has perceived,
no eye has seen any God besides you,
who works for those who wait for him.

(Isaiah 64:1, 2b-4)

Through God's favor and the willingness of an unassuming young girl from Nazareth, the world's long-awaited prayers could be answered. But will Mary stick to her own plans for her life, or will she step into God's surprising and uncertain future? Gabriel's announcement and call on Mary's life demands a response. Her answer is simple and direct: "Here am I, the servant of the Lord; let it be with me according to your word" (Luke 1:38).

Mary's plans for an ordinary life are broken by an extraordinary call. Her yes becomes the doorway for God's blessing.

"Here Am I"

When Abraham said yes to God, he was eventually blessed with a son whose descendants gave life to the twelve tribes of Israel. Because of his yes, Jesus was born centuries later in Bethlehem. Because of one man's yes we, too, are blessed to know the reality of God's love in our own lives and the depth of love God has for all of God's children. And our yes to God also becomes the doorway to God's blessings; we are blessed to answer yes to our own call in order to be a blessing to others.

Mary's answer to her surprising and unexpected call, "Here am I, the servant of the Lord," was her yes to God. "Here am I." Mary was in good company when she said those words. It was the response of many of the great prophets when they unexpectedly heard God's call. One of my seminary professors reminded his students that when God calls, the only appropriate response is "Here I am!" When Moses approaches the burning bush on Mount Sinai, God calls him by name, just as the angel called Mary by name: "Moses, Moses!" And he answered, "Here I am" (Exodus 3:4). His yes to God led the enslaved Israelites out of captivity in Egypt. The young boy Samuel says, "Here I am!" when God surprises him by calling his name three times in the middle of the night (1 Samuel 3:4-9). When God cries out to Isaiah, "Whom shall I send, and who will go for us?" Isaiah answers, "Here am I; send me!" (Isaiah 6:8).

We are all called by God, perhaps to be a spouse, parent, accountant, doctor, teacher, docent at the museum, or volunteer at the food bank. And sometimes while we're living one call, God interrupts our life and places an additional or totally different call on us. What are the ways in which you've said yes to God? Were your life's plans interrupted by this? Perhaps you, like Abraham, were asked to move from one state or country to another. Maybe you had pauses to your career that on the surface appeared to be devastating, but, in the end, became a blessing. Maybe you, too, longed to be a parent and finally received that blessing after long battles with infertility. Perhaps you began in one career or vocation and ended up in an area that you had never imagined. I know that was the case for me.

If you have read any of my other books, you may know that I, from a relatively young age, knew that I wanted to be a teacher, and I was. I taught high school for years and loved it. Then, when my children were born, I sensed God's call to stay home with them. In my mind, that is how I would live out my call: being a mom and volunteering at our church and in various ways in the community until our children graduated from high school. But God had other plans.

When my children were both still quite young, my husband and I sponsored a friend on a spiritual retreat called The Walk to Emmaus. As part of the retreat weekend, we attended a worship service where we prayed for the attendees and ended the service with Communion. Before the service started, the lead minister tapped me on the shoulder and asked, "Would you mind helping me serve Communion?" I was thrilled to do so but was unsure what I was supposed to do or say. So he instructed me, "We are going to serve by intinction. I will break the bread and offer each person a piece of it, saying, 'The body of Christ broken for you.' You will hold the chalice, and as each person dips their bread into the cup, you will say, 'The blood of Christ given for you.'"

As each person came forward to receive Communion, and I kept repeating, almost as if it became a mantra, "The blood of Christ given for you," something surreal happened. I had the clearest thought and sensed God saying to me, "This is what you're supposed to be doing." That night I kept wondering, *What does this mean? Does this mean I'm supposed to be more involved in volunteering in the church? Does it mean that I'm supposed to go to seminary to be become a better-educated Sunday school teacher and small-group leader? Or does it mean that I'm supposed to go to seminary in order to become an ordained minister?* It took an enormous amount of discernment to figure out just what "this" meant, but I knew then that God was calling me to something new, and I knew that it was going to create a major disruption in the plans I had for myself and my family.

God placed a call on my life and led me into an uncertain future that I could never have imagined on my own, nor could I have imagined in the long run what a blessing it would bring to me, my family, and hopefully to those I served. That call led me to people I would have never known otherwise. It stretched me professionally in ways I could never have imagined. It led me to the love of writing and teaching Bible studies. And in a circuitous way, it led me to my present call in walking alongside and advocating for immigrants who might be anxious, afraid, or suffering in our country right now.

Saying "here am I" to God is almost always disruptive, and it doesn't mean that life is always going to be rosy (Mary's life certainly wasn't), but it will be blessed. And in living out your call, you will bring God's blessings to others as well, as they see the love of God made manifest in you.

Mary as Prophet

Answering a call often places both the blessing and the weight of another on our shoulders. When I first accepted the role of executive minister at the church I served in Dallas for twenty years, I was excited to become "pastor to the pastors," as my senior minister dubbed it, and offer oversight to various departments in the church. But with that also came the responsibility of navigating disagreements between staff members or between congregants and staff. It also meant that I often acted as the customer service department, trying to be an understanding ear or soothe ruffled feathers among church members. Answering the call of preacher also meant that sometimes God required I speak a prophetic word in my sermons—words that I knew would make some people uncomfortable or angry.

The word *prophetic* often conjures up images of a fortune teller sitting in front of a crystal ball, gazing into the future. Prophets in the Old Testament were not fortune tellers, though they did sometimes predict future events. Their main function was to speak for God and call God's people to turn from ways that were not pleasing to God. They were to call people to turn back toward God and the ways in which God desired them to live. Many prophets in the Old Testament called people to turn from idolatry, from cheating their employees, from withholding food and goods from the poor, the widow, the orphan. Prophets had harsh words for God's people who mistreated their neighbors or aliens who lived among them.

The list of ways God's prophets called God's people to task is long, because the list of ways we stray from God's intended path for our lives is endless. Prophets remind people of what God has called them to do, and most of the time it is to "do justice and to love kindness and to walk humbly with your God" (Micah 6:8). Jesus himself used his prophetic voice to call us to do justice, love mercy, and walk humbly with our God by reminding us that the love of God and love of neighbor are the core of the law (Matthew 22:37-39). In Jesus's estimation, we can't love God well, we can't love him well, if we don't love and care for our neighbor (Matthew 25:31-46; Luke 10:25-37).

The prophet's role of offering critique and warning often drew the ire of those to whom they were speaking. Amos spoke against Israel for their religious arrogance and apparent lack of concern for justice, oppressing the poor and needy, and was run out of town (Amos 4:1; 7:10-17). Jeremiah faced constant hostility for his stinging words of reproach. He was routinely mocked, beaten, and imprisoned and was once thrown into a well because of his rebukes (Jeremiah 38). Isaiah faced intense ire for his condemnation of idolatry, calls for social justice, and rebukes against misguided political alliances made by Israel's leaders. John the Baptist was beheaded for speaking out against King Herod's immorality (Matthew 14:1-12). Prophets' lives, as they were answering God's call, could be filled with danger and struggle.

The call placed on Mary would become, as pastor Ashley Cleere Cook writes, "an honor yoked with struggle."[1] I love that description, for it fits all of our lives. Mary would experience the struggle of facing the stigma of a baby born too early, or possibly the doubts of feeling inadequate, even while she reveled in the favor of nurturing in her womb the Son of God. She would, one day, alongside the deep love and pride she felt for her son, also face the unbearable heartbreak of watching him die for you and me. With her yes to God also came the blessing and weight of offering her own prophetic word (that we will discuss soon), that no doubt still makes people uncomfortable, and sometimes angry, and an eventual piercing of her own soul.

Luke's Gospel tells us that just after Mary hears of Elizabeth's miraculous pregnancy and answers, "Here am I," to God's call on her life, she "went with haste" to visit her relative Elizabeth in the hill country of Judea (Luke 1:39). We don't know the cause of her feeling the need to leave immediately to make this ninety-mile journey. Perhaps she surmised it would be good to get out of town for a while in the aftermath of her surprising news. Maybe she thought that the only person in the world who could truly understand what was happening to her would be Elizabeth. It could be that she wanted to go help Elizabeth in her last months of pregnancy and share in her joy. They could also offer support to each other. Perhaps all of the above were sources for her desire to go so quickly. So she "went with haste."

When Mary steps through the threshold of Elizabeth's home after what would have been an arduous, days-long journey, Mary greets Elizabeth, and Elizabeth's baby leaps in her womb, revealing that Gabriel's announcement about Elizabeth's baby has come to fruition: Elizabeth's child will be filled with the Holy Spirit from his mother's womb (Luke 1:15). Elizabeth, too, is overcome by the Holy Spirit (Luke 1:41) and sings her own prophetic words to Mary:

> *Blessed are you among women, and blessed is the fruit of your womb. And why has this happened to me, that the mother of my Lord comes to me? For as soon as I heard the sound of your greeting, the child in my womb leaped for joy. And blessed is she who believed that there would be a fulfillment of what was spoken to her by the Lord.*
>
> *(Luke 1:42-45)*

Elizabeth hadn't known about Mary's pregnancy. And yet, through the Holy Spirit, she now knows. She knows that Mary is carrying Elizabeth's Lord, our Lord, the Lord that the world has been waiting for and praying for, the Lord we still wait and pray for. Can you imagine how comforting it must have been for Mary for Elizabeth to confirm what Gabriel had shared with her? She *was* favored. She *was* blessed for many reasons, but among those is that she believed in the words of Gabriel. She put her trust in his words and in her call. The confidence that came from Elizabeth's affirming words prompts Mary's heart and lips to pour out her own Spirit-filled and prophetic song of praise to God.

Mary's Prophetic Words

Mary's song in Luke 1, often called the Magnificat, is named for the first word of the song in Latin:

My soul magnifies [Latin: magnificat*] the Lord,*
and my spirit rejoices in God my Savior,
for he has looked with favor on the lowly state of his servant.
Surely from now on all generations will call me blessed,
for the Mighty One has done great things for me,
and holy is his name;
indeed, his mercy is for those who fear him
from generation to generation.
He has shown strength with his arm;
he has scattered the proud in the imagination of their hearts.
He has brought down the powerful from their thrones
and lifted up the lowly;
he has filled the hungry with good things
and sent the rich away empty.
He has come to the aid of his child Israel,
in remembrance of his mercy,
according to the promise he made to our ancestors,
to Abraham and to his descendants forever.

(Luke 1:46-55)

How do these words make you feel? What images and ideas do they bring to mind? When I read Mary's prophetic words, I experience a range of ideas and emotions: gratitude, hopefulness, and a sense of connection to Mary and the teachings of Jesus.

The Magnificat celebrates God's goodness to Mary (and us) by recalling God's faithfulness to Israel. It was a covenantal faithfulness that bound God's mighty deeds of the past to the new thing that God was doing, and continues to do, in the world through the birth of Jesus the Christ. Also, throughout the Gospels, including Luke's, we see Jesus saying that those who want to be first must be last; those who want to be exalted must first humble themselves. His kingdom is for those who look not to be served but to serve, and Mary seems to understand this even before Christ's birth. More broadly, the Magnificat echoes themes emphasized in Luke's Gospel, particularly God's concern for the lowly, the hungry, the oppressed and disenfranchised, and God's judgment on the greedy and power hungry. John Wesley, the founder of the Methodist tradition, numbers Mary among the prophets by observing that she spoke "under a prophetic impulse."[2]

If we're honest, we probably feel uncomfortable reading some of Mary's prophetic words. Even if we're not rich but are merely financially comfortable, even if we don't consider ourselves powerful but know we're not powerless, we might think Mary's words are directed at us.

The lifting up of the lowly or humble and the tearing down of oppressive regimes or those in power is a common theme in the Hebrew Scriptures, extending all the way to the story of God's deliverance of the Israelites from slavery in Egypt. We can agree that for the sake of justice in the world, that is a good thing. While most of us do not sit on thrones, many of us can wield power or privilege in one way or another. And those of us who live in the United States today, compared to people in many other countries as well as people from different time periods, could be considered wealthy if we consider a broad perspective. And I don't know about you, but being sent away hungry is not appealing to me. It is not something that I have hoped or prayed for.

But let's take a look at the scripture from a slightly different angle. Those of us who have even a little bit of power, who have more than enough materially, can humble *ourselves* to help bring justice to those who experience injustice; we can wield our influence to seek the justice God desires for others. We can, with our power, act as a voice for those whose voices are ignored or go unheard. We can humble ourselves and share the blessings we have been given, or we can *be* humbled.

Jesus's first act of ministry in Luke's Gospel was to open the scroll of Isaiah in his hometown synagogue and read these words:

The Spirit of the Lord is upon me,
because he has anointed me
to bring good news to the poor.
He has sent me to proclaim release to the captives
and recovery of sight to the blind,
to set free those who are oppressed,
to proclaim the year of the Lord's favor.
(Luke 4:18-19)

Jesus announced in his coming that the prophetic words of Isaiah would be fulfilled. So would his mother's. The sad thing is that the good people who heard his words felt uncomfortable being reminded, by their hometown boy, of how they were to live before God. So, like the people did to Amos in his day, they ran Jesus out of town (Luke 4:29). Prophetic voices are not always appreciated.

Mary's words may be disturbing or unsettling to some readers today. However, the Magnificat reminds us not so much that the rich and powerful are excluded but that the lowly, the luckless, the friendless, the sick, the marginalized are all to be exalted, and those who humble themselves will help lift them up. At long last, they will be treated on earth like the beloved children of God that they are.

What God Does

In the Magnificat, Mary tells us that God

has looked with favor on the lowly state of his servant...
for the Mighty One ***has*** *done great things for me...*
has *scattered the proud...*
has *brought down the powerful...*
has *filled the hungry.*

(Luke 1:48-49, 51-53, emphasis added)

Even though Mary is in a time of expectation and waiting, with Jesus still in her womb, she astonishingly speaks these powerful words not about what God *will* do but about what God *has* done. The focus here is not on actions that are complete and finished in the long-distant past, nor on actions that are, hopefully, still to come. Rather, it is about who God has shown Godself to be or, in other words, who God was, is, and will be.

What we see in Mary's words is a world where there is no hierarchy, where everyone is full, where everyone has a place at the table. It is a vision of God's kingdom on earth as it is in heaven. It is a kingdom of justice and care, a kingdom where the love of God is evident to everyone.

I don't know about you, but there are days when I look around at some of the events in our world and ask, "Where is

God's kingdom in all of this? Where *is* the Kingdom?" Where is the Kingdom in the middle of those being harmed by wars and human trafficking, the asylum seekers I see every week who are being detained and deported even when they have done all that is required by law? Where is the Kingdom when there is so much evil, injustice, and oppression occurring around us?

Mary is poor. She is pregnant out of wedlock. For a teenage girl, there's almost nothing more frightening. So in the back of her mind she could see the potential of being cast off, perhaps with no hope of being able to care for herself and her child.

That's what we might see through our eyes. But Mary sees "God has." And if Mary can do that, so can we. Not only *can* we do that, Mary prophetically calls us to do that, to believe, like her, that God *has*—right here and now.[3]

We can see what God has done when refugees from war-torn areas are welcomed into other countries that offer them asylum and care. We can see what God has done when the hungry are fed in our communities through the work of our churches and local food banks. We can see what God has done when community pressure prevents an immigration detention center from being built in our backyards. You can see what God has done when a friend or neighbor lifts you up, whether in spirit or physically, during a difficult time in life. While we can get discouraged at what has not yet happened, we are called to live into Mary's vision that "God *has*." It was in part this orientation that made it possible for Mary to respond to God's call how she did, taking on the unexpected challenges laid before her with the confidence of someone who deeply trusts in God's loving faithfulness.

Perhaps, during the next four weeks in Advent, we are called to clearing our field of vision and perception so that we can see, understand, experience, and live into what God has done more fully. The more we can show how God has lifted up the lowly and oppressed and fed the hungry, the more evident "God has" can become to those who wear the blinders of injustice and oppression and lack mercy and compassion.

In short, we are called to perceive "God has" in the same way the mother of Jesus did. So, in response to Mary's story, message, and call, which is integral to our Advent story, let us accept our own calls and say, as Mary did, "Here am I, the servant of the Lord; let it be with me according to your word" (Luke 1:38). And may we, like Mary, not be distracted and disheartened when plans change and the life we thought was secure is upended. Let us bring into the world the new thing that God wants to do in the world through us, so that what we know to be true—"God has"—becomes a reality for all people.

JOSEPH

The Surprise of Trust

CHAPTER 2

CHAPTER 2

Joseph

The Surprise of Trust

Now the birth of Jesus the Messiah took place in this way. When his mother Mary had been engaged to Joseph, but before they lived together, she was found to be pregnant from the Holy Spirit. Her husband Joseph, being a righteous man and unwilling to expose her to public disgrace, planned to divorce her quietly. But just when he had resolved to do this, an angel of the Lord appeared to him in a dream and said, "Joseph, son of David, do not be afraid to take Mary as your wife, for the child conceived in her is from the Holy Spirit. She will bear a son, and you are to name him Jesus, for he will save his people from their sins."

(Matthew 1:18-22)

A shoot shall come out from the stump of Jesse,
and a branch shall grow out of his roots.
The spirit of the Lord shall rest on him,
the spirit of wisdom and understanding,
the spirit of counsel and might,
the spirit of knowledge and the fear of the Lord.

(Isaiah 11:1-2)

Have you ever had a moment in your life when there was no question as to what you were going to do? You were resolved to push through with a plan of action. Only you found that plan thwarted not by any act of malintent on another person's part but perhaps by the interaction and discussion with someone who caused you to change your mind?

When our daughter was four years old, we moved into a new house. It was a real fixer-upper but had a great deal of potential. We knew that we would eventually replace all of the carpets, repaint all of the walls, and refinish the hardwood floors, but the work would be done in stages that would take a year or more. One day, just after we had moved in, I found Caroline sitting on the floor of her new room surrounded by markers, as she was brilliantly placing the finishing touches on a grand mural . . . which happened to be on her carpet. The artwork covered at least two-thirds of the floor's surface. I was shocked, to say the least. She had never done anything like this before. She was a rule follower and had always colored or used markers on the usual places we taught her to draw on. While I knew the carpet would be replaced in the near future, I also knew my husband and I couldn't let this action go without severe consequences. She needed to learn that this could *never* happen again. The markers were taken away while she had a significant time-out in her room, allowing her father and me the opportunity to discuss what we were going to do. We came up with a plan that we were resolved to implement.

Afterward, we invited Caroline to join us for a discussion of her actions. We asked her questions like, "Why would you do such a thing? You do know that you're not allowed to color on your carpet, don't you?" and, "Carpet is extremely expensive, and you know this is very serious, don't you?" She offered all the right answers to our questions. My husband then sat Caroline on his lap and said, "Caroline, Mom and I have been talking about what kind of consequences you should have for what you've done, but before we tell you what we think we should do, I want to hear from you. What would you do if you were us? What do you think we should do?" She thought for a moment, and then looked up at her dad and said, "Well…we could make up a song!" I had to turn my head so that Caroline couldn't see me laughing, and Ike was biting his lip, trying to keep a straight and stern face. Needless to say, our resolve was broken and those severe consequences mellowed somewhat.

This story, and the feelings my husband and I experienced when we saw a room full of destroyed carpet, can't begin to equate to the anguish Joseph experienced at what he perceived as a complete betrayal by his bride-to-be that would destroy their relationship and future. However, like us, Joseph had a change in resolve as a result of what was said to him. But in Joseph's situation, it wasn't much of a conversation; it was a one-sided communication. He must decide whether he's going to trust the source and then if he is going to trust Mary and whatever she may have told him about the baby's conception.

A Disruption from Mary

We aren't privy to the conversation Mary has with Joseph before he becomes "resolved" to quietly dismiss, or divorce, her. At some point, when she realizes she is pregnant, Mary has to bravely sit down with Joseph to have a difficult conversation. Even though she knows the truth about the events surrounding the baby's conception, she must be more than a little concerned that Joseph might not believe the unbelievable. When she begins their conversation with the word *angel*, continues by telling him that her pregnancy is of the Holy Spirit, and finishes by saying that the child she is carrying will be the Davidic king, the Messiah, that the world has been waiting for, my guess is that this news is more than Joseph can bear. I can also imagine Mary saying something like this to Joseph: "Please, please know that I love you. I would never betray you. It is my prayer and my hope that you and I can raise this God-ordained child together, that together we can serve our Lord by being incredible parents to this precious baby." Joseph has just been confronted with an unwanted surprise and disruption of his plans for a bright future with Mary.

Again, we don't know what Joseph's response to Mary might have been. Did he think Mary was out of her mind, that she obviously was not mentally stable and actually believed her own outrageous story? Did he think Mary's words were a complete fabrication to cover up an affair in hopes that Joseph would accept her words as true and raise another man's child as his own? That would save her from completely disgracing her parents' and her own reputation. But there would be talk soon enough. And then what about his reputation? Would he be complicit in a lie in order to maintain the betrothal covenant between them and their families? How could Mary do this to him?

It's not difficult for us to imagine Joseph's heartbreak, rage, and indignity at hearing Mary's words. It's also not difficult to imagine Joseph responding with words similar to these: "Listen to what you've just said, Mary! Do you really expect me to believe this? Would *you* believe you? I can't fathom that after all of the plans we've made, after we've pledged ourselves to each other, after I've been breaking my back to build a home for the two of us, that you would disgrace me and our families like this. I just don't understand. I never thought you would be capable of such a betrayal. I need time to think about what I'm going to do."

Justice Tempered by Mercy

The scripture above tells us that Joseph is a "righteous man," which means he keeps the law of Moses meticulously. Joseph, like my daughter, is a rule follower who is not prone to coloring outside the boundaries of God's law. And he certainly would expect the same from his wife. In Joseph's mind, there was only one thing he could do since Mary had obviously broken their covenant: He must divorce her. But how would he go about doing this? In the kindest way possible, it seems (another reason he is righteous). By this example we see that Joseph's sense of justice is tempered by mercy, as is God's. For throughout the Bible, we are told and we see examples of how God is "slow to anger and abounding in steadfast love. / . . . He does not deal with us according to our sins / nor repay us according to our iniquities" (Psalm 103:8, 10). God is not only gracious and merciful but also "good to all, / and his compassion is over all that he has made" (Psalm 145:9).

God's justice tempered by mercy is made evident through story after story of the lives of God's people. From the very beginning, we see God judging Cain for murdering his brother Abel, banishing him from his fields to become an aimless wanderer, but also tempering this justice by placing a mark on Cain preventing anyone from killing him (Genesis 4).

After leading the Israelites out of slavery in Egypt, God causes them to wander through the wilderness for forty years due to their many acts of disobedience but continues to graciously provide them with manna and quail for food, water that miraculously flows from rocks, and protection from their enemies. God eventually leads their descendants, through Moses and Joshua, to the Promised Land (see Numbers 14:13-34 for a good summary of this). God's justice is always tempered with mercy out of God's deep love and compassion for God's people. Joseph exhibits this kind of righteousness as he resolves to divorce Mary, but to do so quietly to spare her any further embarrassment or harm.

To be righteous is to live "rightly"—to live according to the will of God, God's laws, and God's character. That includes living as the prophet Micah, who Joseph may have been familiar with, decreed: "[God] has told you, O mortal, what is good, / and what does the LORD require of you / but to do justice and to love kindness / and to walk humbly with your God?" (Micah 6:8). The word "kindness" here is *hesed* in Hebrew. *Hesed* is also translated as "mercy" or "faithfulness." Here, it depicts God's requirement for people to live justly and show mercy, or kindness, to those in need. When *hesed* is used to describe God, it refers to God's never-changing, continuous faithfulness to God's people. This is the kind of faithfulness, mercy, and kindness we are to show others as well, the mercy that we can only offer through God's own faithfulness to us. This is the kind of justice tempered by mercy Joseph resolves to offer Mary.

Four Gospels, Two Very Different Birth Stories

Only two of the four Gospels include the birth narrative of Jesus: Matthew and Luke. In Luke's Gospel, the story of the angel's visit to Mary, the announcement that she will conceive a son, her visit to Elizabeth, and Mary's song of praise to God for her pregnancy comprises thirty verses. If we look at the familiar passages about Jesus's birth in Luke—Jesus being born in Bethlehem because of the census, being laid in a manger because there was no room in the inn, and the shepherds' visit to the Holy Family afterward—that adds another twenty verses. So Luke commits fifty verses to the announcement of Jesus's conception and his birth. Matthew, on the other hand, offers us two chapters of stories about Jesus's conception and events following his birth but only a brief but powerful seven verses of his actual birth story.

Matthew omits so much of what we find endearing in Luke's Gospel. There is no mention of an angelic visitor to Elizabeth's husband announcing the coming of their son, John the Baptist, or to Mary. There's no manger or shepherds watching over their flocks by night; no chorus of angels heralding the good news for all people of the birth of a king. Matthew offers us a quite different story, one in which the newborn king is not visited by shepherds and heralded by angels but whose birth is recognized by foreign astronomers—the wise men, or magi. Luke's birth narrative tends to focus on Jesus's conception and arrival from Mary's perspective. Matthew's story of Jesus's birth highlights

Joseph's involvement. It's likely the authors of Matthew and Luke were unfamiliar with the other's versions of the Nativity. It is well acknowledged by many scholars that Matthew and Luke wrote independently of each other, without knowing the details of each other's work.

Many people have no idea that the two Gospels vary so markedly in what they tell us (and don't tell us) about the birth of Jesus. Perhaps that's because everything gets combined in our most popular cultural representations. In our Christmas pageants, and in our home Nativity sets, we find the wise men with their extravagant gifts rubbing shoulders with the shepherds, lambs draped across their shoulders, all vying for space among the cattle, donkeys, and camels, to see the newborn babe lying in a manger. I'm not disparaging the fact that our culture has merged these two vastly different Nativity narratives. Doing so has provided us with a deep sense of warmth and affection around the birth of Jesus and has helped our children (and us) remember the broad outlines of the Gospel narratives. However, reading the stories independently of each other offers us a glimpse into the theological emphasis of each author.

Even though their infancy narratives differ in many respects, Matthew and Luke agree on several points:

- The parents of Jesus are named Mary and Joseph who are betrothed but have not yet lived together or had relations with each other (Matthew 1:18; Luke 1:27, 34).
- Joseph is of the lineage of King David (Matthew 1:16, 20; Luke 1:27, 32; 2:4).

- An angel announces the upcoming birth of the child (Matthew 1:20-23; Luke 1:30-35).
- The child is not conceived by Mary through relations with her husband, but through the Holy Spirit (Matthew 1:18, 20, 23, 25; Luke 1:34-35).
- The angel that announces the coming birth of the child also instructs that the baby is to be named Jesus (Matthew 1:21; Luke 1:31).
- The angel states that Jesus is to be a Savior (Matthew 1:21; Luke 2:11).
- Jesus is born after his parents come to live together (Matthew 1:24-25; Luke 2:5-6).
- Jesus's birth is historically related to the reign of Herod the Great (Matthew 2:1; Luke 1:5).
- Jesus is raised in Nazareth (Matthew 2:23; Luke 2:39).[1]

Recall from the previous chapter that the stories of women's inability to conceive in Luke's Gospel were intended to help the audience relate this story to other similar ones in the Bible. They would remember and know that the God who had intervened in the lives of Abraham and Sarah, Hannah, Rebekah, and Jacob and Rachel was now miraculously working in the lives of Elizabeth and Zechariah, and Mary and Joseph, to bring about God's purposes on earth. The same God was capable of working miraculously in their lives as well. For nothing is impossible with God. The Davidic king that had been promised a thousand years before, the one the world had been praying for, has been born to and for them. Also, the story of Elizabeth, and how God caused her to miraculously conceive a son through her husband, helped prepare the first-century listener of Luke's Gospel to hear of the conception of Jesus through the Holy Spirit. Lest we forget, *nothing* is impossible with God.

Similarly, Matthew uses Joseph and Jesus's lineage to offer an equally important message, but for a different audience. For as many as three decades following Jesus's death and resurrection, his followers were accepted as one of the many groups within Judaism, just as we acknowledge Wesleyans, Calvinists, and Lutherans as groups, or denominations, within Christianity. However, Matthew's Gospel was written sometime around AD 80 or 90, long after the destruction of the temple by Rome in AD 70, to a mostly Jewish community that was experiencing its own disruptions—not by an angel but from those within the Jewish tradition.

It is likely that during the first century, some Jewish Christians were expelled from synagogues for their insistence on Jesus's identity as the Son of God. Jewish Christians and non-Christian Jews were beginning to focus on their differences rather than their many shared beliefs—love of God and love of neighbor being paramount among those. The Christian communities, still rooted in the Scriptures and history of Israel, were also experiencing a rapid influx of Gentiles (or non-Jews) into their circles of faith, as news of Jesus spread throughout the Roman Empire. They began to wrestle with how to balance their own faith practices and traditions with an emerging faith that welcomed people from outside of their traditions who might have little knowledge of their Scriptures.

Pressing questions surfaced for them: Should Gentiles be required to be circumcised (it was the sign of God's covenant with Israel after all)? Should newcomers, or any of them for that matter, now adhere to Israel's dietary laws? Should the laws of Israel that the Jewish Christians clung to with great love be abolished? Would this growing community have to divorce itself from its long-held traditions, history, and Scriptures in order to remain a part of and accommodate this ever-growing Christian movement? According to Matthew, the clear and solid answer is a resounding no.

While this may seem obvious to you as a Christian today, for we of course hold dear the Hebrew Scriptures and the stories within them, there was hot debate, for instance, over circumcision and food laws—effectively, whether a Gentile would need to become Jewish in order to enter the faith. God had surprised the world with the birth of Christ, and there was a lot of work to do to figure out what his life and teachings meant for those who wanted to follow him. In each of the four Gospels, Jesus instructs the disciples to take his message into the world and share it with others. Precisely how to do this and what this entailed was not spelled out, and those early disciples had to discern their own answers.

Our Christian history is teeming with examples of trying to balance old traditions and scriptural interpretations with the new thing to which God is calling us—and calling us to trust, like Joseph did. In the past, the church struggled with the debate over the use of icons, the ownership of slaves, and the ordination of women (a debate that continues in some denominations). Currently, many churches are in debate over the acceptance, marriage, and ordination of LGBTQ+ people. The struggle of balancing the old with the new is as old as, well, Jesus talking about trying to pour new wine into old wineskins (Matthew 9:17; Mark 2:22; Luke 5:37-39). In essence, old rigid wineskins cannot hold the new fermenting and expanding wine. When God is doing something new through Jesus's teachings, they can't be forced into old rigid systems, but those systems and structures can provide a sense of security and continuity with what has gone before.

What is obvious is that there will never be a time when there is no debate or struggle about how to maintain and change the traditions of the church, because with every cultural shift, God calls us to new ways of being the body of Christ in and for the world while we continue to honor and love our heritage. The heritage isn't jettisoned. What comes next is an extension and perhaps fulfillment of the past. Understanding the past empowers growth for the future. Today, as Christians have throughout the history of the church, we need to remember that traditions may change, but God's love and guidance are constant and abiding.

That was good news to the Jewish Christians who were also wondering if they would be able to continue melding their Jewish heritage with the new thing (the new, surprising disruption) that was happening in their Christian faith. They wondered if the Torah, the law, the prophets, and the patriarchs and kings of Israel would still be able to hold a place of reverence in this new faith of theirs. For Matthew, the clear and resounding answer is yes. And his yes begins with a genealogy that will conclude with a blessing, not only for Mary and Joseph, but for all people.

Genealogies (Really) Matter

The birth narrative of Jesus begins in Matthew 1:18-25. But the author of Matthew intentionally sets up the birth of Jesus in the first seventeen verses of the book by including a genealogy as an introduction. What? A genealogy? You might be thinking that no author, no journalist, no novelist would *ever* begin a book or an article that they hoped would be read by anyone with a long genealogy, but Matthew does! The times I've preached on this text (Matthew 1:1-17) and stood in the pulpit reading it aloud, "An account of the genealogy of Jesus the Messiah, the son of David, the son of Abraham. Abraham was the father of Isaac, and Isaac the father of Jacob, . . . and Obed the father of Jesse, and Jesse the father of King David . . ." I could see people beginning to panic, especially the ones who knew their Bible. I could almost read their thoughts. *She's not going to recite all the generations from Abraham to Jesus, is she? Oh no! She is!*

And the thing is, if you were Jewish and living in the time after Jesus had died, and you had questions about who Jesus was and why he might be relevant to you and your faith, you would be highly interested in the opening words of Matthew's Gospel. You would have recognized the patriarch names of the past, the famous kings like David and Solomon, but you might have puzzled over names that were long forgotten, like photos of relatives that your grandparents could name with ease but you couldn't place at all.

Your ears would perk up when you heard the familiar names of the past—of *your* past. You would be reminded with the calling of each name the checkered past of Israel. The good, the bad, the scandalous, and the forgettable all were beneficiaries of God's blessings and faithfulness, even in the midst of their foibles, misdeeds, scandals, and challenges. And at the end of the reading, you would be perhaps surprised but also excited to know that the last person mentioned in that genealogy, Jesus—your Jesus—is the fulfillment of all that God had been doing in the life of Israel since God first appeared to Abraham and told him he would become the father of a multitude of nations. You, too, are part of that great heritage and God's plan for an incredible new future through Jesus the Christ (Romans 4:16). This future began at his birth and begins anew for us each day.

Many have said that Matthew's genealogy of Jesus contains his purpose for the whole of the Gospel. In a sense, it is a Gospel genealogy that contains a few surprises and unexpected turns of its own. Matthew doesn't sanitize Jesus's lineage. All kinds of people are included: rich and poor, righteous and devious (and some who were both at different times in their lives—like David, who was a man after God's own heart bus who was also an adulterer responsible for the death of his mistress's husband), royal and peasant, those with questionable backgrounds and the pedigreed. God *chose,* and was able to use, all of these people to play a role in bringing forth God's own Son into the world. God used them to bring about God's purposes in the past and in the future. It was all these types of people whom Jesus included in his ministry and welcomed to his table, whom he healed, who became his followers and changed the world. That means God chooses you, too, no matter if your past is pristine or as checkered as Israel's, to bring about God's purposes in the world. If you've ever worried that something in your past has made your relationship with God or your usefulness to God a nonstarter, Matthew's genealogy of Jesus puts all of that to rest. You, too, are vital in bearing Christ in this world, just as Mary and Joseph were.

Matthew's Gospel points to Jesus's inclusiveness in another way. If you've read other genealogies in the Bible, you've probably noticed that most of them do not mention women, but Matthew does. And the women's names he mentions are eyebrow-raising: Tamar (Genesis 38) disguises herself as a prostitute and seduces her father-in-law in order to become pregnant. Rahab (Joshua 2:1-21; 6:22-25) is a prostitute who offers her home as a hideout for Hebrew spies planning the invasion of Jericho as they settle into the Promised Land. Ruth (Ruth 2–4) is a Moabite woman who is loyal to her mother-in-law, Naomi. She presents herself at night to Boaz in hopes of procuring redemption and a male heir for the two childless widows. "The wife of Uriah," whom we know as Bathsheba, is taken by King David from her husband (David's loyal Hittite army commander) and becomes his mistress, and later wife, who gives birth to King Solomon. All of these women are Gentiles, or strongly associated with Gentile nations, and have unusual, and sometimes scandalous, birth stories.

These unexpected inclusions in Matthew's genealogy prepare us to hear the story of the Gentile wise men who appear to King Herod to announce the birth of a new king. And more broadly, these Gentile women foreshadow Jesus's own acceptance and inclusion of Gentiles so that Matthew's community knows that they, too, should be willing to open their minds and arms to those not like themselves. For since the time of Abraham, God has said that one day all nations would turn to God because of Abraham. He was blessed to be a blessing to all people and all nations (Genesis 12:1-4; 22:18; Isaiah 49:6). Like many aspects of the Christian story, God is doing something surprising, new, and unexpected that, from another point of view, is entirely in line with what came before.

These four women's inclusion in Matthew's genealogy also prepares us, much as Elizabeth's conception story did in Luke, to hear of Mary's own unusual conception story told by the angel to Joseph. When Matthew's audience heard Mary's name read in this genealogy in 1:16 ("Jacob the father of Joseph the husband of Mary, who bore Jesus, who is called the Messiah"), they would have been clued in that they were about to hear about Joseph's and her own exciting and unusual birth story.

Matthew's incorporation of Jesus's genealogy affirms Jesus's gospel message of inclusion, grace, love, and redemption. It also affirms Jesus's true identity from beginning to end: He is the Messiah, the son of David, the son of Abraham. He is the shoot that Isaiah predicted would come out of the stump of Jesse, King David's father (Isaiah 11:1-2). And Joseph is chosen by God to be a vital part of his story. So, too, are you.

The Surprise of Interruption, Trust, and a Gender Reveal

I've recently become a grandmother. It is true that grandparenting is the most fun and greatest calling in life. My daughter gave birth to a beautiful baby girl, Elizabeth (sometimes we call her Betty after her great-grandmother), just a few months ago. She has the most gorgeous steel blue eyes gifted to her by her father, and the porcelain, china doll complexion and strawberry blonde hair of her mother. What I find fascinating about her birth story is that, contrary to people in generations past, her mom and dad had the ability to know almost as quickly as Zechariah and Elizabeth, and Mary and Joseph, when they were pregnant and what the gender of their baby would be due to advances in medical technology.

Betty's mom and dad surprised us the summer before last when they came for a visit to Colorado with the announcement that they were going to have a baby. They were still on cloud nine because they had just discovered this good news the night before. When they shared the exciting news with us, we laughed and cried and hugged everyone in the room. We repeated all of the emotions and hugging all over again, several times. Then we all got on a video call and shared the glorious news with our son and his wife and repeated the laughing and crying—and I forgot to mention, cheering—again! It was one of the most joyous days of all of our lives.

About eight weeks later, our families were all gathered in our daughter and son-in-law's home, where we found ourselves, in unison, biting into our very own cupcake. It was a race to see who could devour their cupcake first, for the cream filling inside would either contain blue or pink icing depending on the gender of the coming baby. How could they know so quickly that they were both pregnant and going to have a baby girl (pink icing!) in what seemed like no time at all? I'm going to date myself, but when I was pregnant with my children, it took a little while to discover you were pregnant, and if you were lucky, when you were five months along, if the baby was cooperating with the sonogram, the doctor *might* be able to tell you the gender. All of this good news in such rapid succession was gleefully overwhelming and also seemed to us a medical miracle. The surprises just kept coming.

I need to pause here to interject some interesting information. Joseph has a namesake in the Old Testament who was a bit of a dreamer, so to speak. That is, the story of Joseph in Genesis 37–44 has both fascinating dreams that foretell his future as a leader to whom his brothers will one day bow before, and the ability to interpret the dreams of others. His gift of interpreting dreams takes him from a life of imprisonment and servitude to a life of being Pharaoh's right-hand man in Egypt and a means of salvation for his family. So when we hear of God speaking to Mary's Joseph through an angel in his dream, once again, we are reminded of the goodness and faithfulness of God in the past, who will now be faithful to *this* Joseph in the future.

Joseph, as he lies down for a fitful sleep, resolved to divorce Mary—but in a righteous way, a way that is least hurtful to her—has his own rapid succession of surprises and good news. An angel of the Lord appears to him in a dream and says, "Joseph, son of David, do not be afraid to take Mary as your wife, for the child conceived in her is from the Holy Spirit. She will bear a son, and you are to name him Jesus, for he will save his people from their sins" (Matthew 1:20-21).

In two short sentences offered by an angel in his dreams, Joseph discovers Mary isn't crazy, she isn't an adulteress, and the child she is carrying is of divine origin. Joseph should not be afraid to take her as his wife, to complete their betrothal by taking Mary into his home. He is also given his own exciting gender reveal. This child will be a son and Joseph is to name him Jesus. By bringing Mary into his home and naming the child, Joseph incorporates Jesus into his own lineage, his own genealogy, the genealogy of David and Abraham and everyone else in between and after. This action also indicates his willingness to accept responsibility as Jesus's earthly father. Jesus will be, as Matthew reminds us, the son of David, the son of Abraham, the Messiah—all because Joseph, the dreamer, is willing to believe and trust in the surprising words of the angel.

God Is with Us

Matthew offers the reader an aside that Joseph doesn't hear but that he probably comes to realize: "All this took place to fulfill what had been spoken by the Lord through the prophet [Isaiah]: 'Look, the virgin shall become pregnant and give birth to a son, / and they shall name him Emmanuel,' which means, / 'God is with us'" (Matthew 1:22-23).

God is with us. That is who Jesus is, God with us. In him we can know exactly who God is, what God is really like, how deeply God loves, cares for, and forgives each and every one of God's children. God is with Joseph in his dream, giving him the courage and assurance he needs to take Mary as his wife, and take on the enormous responsibility of being a father to God's Son,

Emmanuel. Joseph goes to sleep with a crushed spirit, dashed hopes for a bright future, a broken heart, and with resolve to divorce Mary and get on with his life as best he can. However, he wakes up with a new resolve: to do what the Lord commanded. He trusts in the message of the angel. He trusts that God will be with him as he reconciles with Mary and takes her into his home, making their marriage official. He knows that he is no longer in control of his life (Was he ever? Are we ever?) and places his trust in the only One who knows the best plan for his, Mary's, and this precious child's life. He trusts that God will lead him to be the best father he can be to this miraculous child, his and Mary's Lord. And when the child is born, Joseph names him as the angel instructs: Jesus.

Don't we sometimes wish we could be like Joseph and have an angel appear in our dreams to tell us how to resolve our seemingly unresolvable problems? I have had a couple of experiences where I thought that God was "speaking" to me very clearly, but more often than not, we have to spend time praying and talking with others who are wise to come to solutions. What we find is that God is with us in our discernment process.

Do you believe that God is with you not only in your dreams or in your mountaintop experiences but all the time? Can you fathom that God is with you when your spirit is crushed, your dreams and hopes are dashed, and your heart is broken? Do you believe God is with you when you feel betrayed? Do you trust that God is with you working for your best and the best of those you love—perhaps working in ways you could never imagine? Do you trust that God is with you when you are pondering what to do next in your life, when you are making hard decisions like Joseph? This is the kind of trust, faith, and belief that Joseph, in his tender righteousness, came to embrace. It is available to you as well.

Have you had a moment like Joseph's when your resolve was challenged and changed by a particular circumstance? Where you felt as if God was speaking to you, guiding you, perhaps through another person? Joseph's life was disrupted by Mary's news. His plans were broken. He made the decision to create a new path for his life, but God's path for Joseph's life was surprisingly different. Then Joseph's life was disrupted, once again, by an angel's surprising words and God's intended path for his life. A life and a path shaped by God's goodness, blessings, and protection. God's intended path for our life may be different from the one we dream of or map out for ourselves, but it always leads to life, joy, and blessings.

Shining Example of a Disciple

One thing I love about Joseph's story is that Joseph never speaks in Matthew's Gospel. Not here and not in the two other times an angel appears to him in his dreams. What Joseph does do is *act*. Joseph awakens from his dream believing in what he has heard—believing in what seems impossible (just as Mary believed what she heard from the angel)—and acts on the angel's commands. Joseph trusts in what God is calling him to do and he *does* it. Joseph puts his faith and trust in the God who is with him and does what he is called to do.

Now, his faith and trust provide a loving and righteous home in which to care for Mary and raise God's coming son. Later, that faith, trust, and action will save the life of the infant Messiah when an angel appears again in his dreams telling Joseph to flee with his wife and the Christ Child to Egypt, for King Herod was set on finding and killing him. After King Herod's death, an angel appears again telling Joseph it's safe to take Jesus back to Israel (Matthew 2:13-23). Joseph never speaks, but in Matthew's Gospel, as they say, his actions speak louder than any words he could have ever uttered. This righteous dreamer is a doer of God's call whenever it appears.

In the Gospel of Matthew, the first human to respond to God's world-changing disruption and intervention in human and world affairs is Joseph. He exemplifies living out the heart and spirit of the law: love of God and love of neighbor as well as justice tempered by mercy. In his actions, Joseph sets the tone for the rest of Matthew's Gospel, as we see Jesus not only citing the letter of the law in the Sermon on the Mount but also imploring his followers to live by the heart, spirit, and intention of the law.

In the Sermon on the Mount, Jesus provides his interpretation of the Law that Moses delivers on Mount Sinai. Jesus speaks what has become called the antitheses: "You have heard that it was said. . . . But I say to you . . ." In them he goes beyond the letter of the law, showing the heart of the law that is grounded in love. For instance, Jesus says, "You have heard that it was said . . . 'You shall not murder' . . . But I say to you that if you are angry with a brother or sister, you will be liable to judgment"

(Matthew 5:21-22a). While this sounds harsh, Jesus knew (and taught) that it is what comes out of our hearts that causes our sinful actions. It is our unrestricted anger that causes murder. Thus, we are to live out the heart of the law, the law of love and mercy, in order to keep the law more deeply. Similarly, consider this teaching: "You have heard that it was said, 'You shall love your neighbor and hate your enemy.' But I say to you: Love your enemies and pray for those who persecute you, so that you may be children of your Father in heaven" (Matthew 5:43-45a). While murder, adultery, and lying are absolute boundaries of the law, the spirit behind it says that hate, lust, and quiet deceit can lead us to sinful actions.

When Jesus comes under scrutiny for feeding his disciples or healing someone on the Sabbath, his actions place him in conflict with religious leaders, and yet he is adamant that his actions are consistent with keeping Sabbath, for the Sabbath was created for the benefit of human beings and not to be a legalistic burden. When we lead with mercy and love, the healing and hunger of human beings take precedent. When he heals on the Sabbath, Jesus is keeping the law of mercy and love.

Thus, in placing his own agenda aside and acting on the angel's command to take Mary as his wife, Joseph becomes the first and prime example of what it means to be a faithful disciple in Matthew's Gospel. He discovers that being righteous often requires that we struggle with complex moral decisions by seeking and listening for God's voice in whatever form it may present itself and then acting on what God calls us to. Sometimes, following that call will put us in conflict with those who insist we live out the letter of the law. Sometimes, we, like Joseph, will struggle when conflict arises within our own soul, our own religious traditions and rules, and God's Spirit calling us down a new and uncertain path and way of living.

On the first Sunday of Advent, in the worship services at the church where I served for twenty years and continue to attend, families or groups of friends are asked to stand near the Advent wreath and read from the Book of Isaiah:

> *The people who walked in darkness*
> *have seen a great light;*
> *those who lived in a land of deep darkness—*
> *on them light has shined. . . .*
> *For a child has been born for us,*
> *a son given to us;*
> *authority rests upon his shoulders,*
> *and he is named*
> *Wonderful Counselor, Mighty God,*
> *Everlasting Father, Prince of Peace. (9:2, 6)*

The absolute best voice for this reading is that of a young child. Call me sentimental, but when I hear a child read this scripture, with the sound of complete innocence and trust ringing through the sanctuary, it brings tears to my eyes every time. Following the scripture reading, someone else from the family or group of friends says these words: "Today we remember the prophets of old, who demanded to be heard, who dared to speak of a child to come, unexpected liberator of the people, vulnerable incarnation of the Holiest of Holies, a new name for God." After the readings, someone from the group prays and then lights the candle of hope on the Advent wreath as a symbol of the prophets who offer us hope, renew our faith, and call us to believe in what yet may be.

Then we sing, in its entirety, the hauntingly moving and beautiful hymn "O Come, O Come, Emmanuel." In every verse resonates the plea, rising from our voices, for God to come to us, to live among us in the flesh, to cheer us, ransom us, to bring us God's justice, to make us one in heart and mind. In the singing of that hymn—every single time—God's presence becomes a palpable and inspiring companion. It's the reason why I mentioned earlier in the book that I wish we would sing this hymn all year long, for we need that kind of hope each and every day. We need the reminder that Emmanuel, God with us, is present with us always.

This is what Matthew, through Joseph's story, is telling us: that the shoot of Jesse, a descendant of David, the one they have been praying and waiting centuries for, has come, and that our response to this good news might require us, like Joseph, to *act*. Joseph doesn't speak, but he is far from passive. Empowered by his trust in God's goodness, truth, and fidelity, in the face of what might otherwise be entirely unbelievable news, he is able to reorient his life to help bring about the new things that God is doing in the world.

THE MAGI

The Surprise of a New Path

CHAPTER 3

CHAPTER 3

The Magi

The Surprise of a New Path

In the time of King Herod, after Jesus was born in Bethlehem of Judea, magi from the east came to Jerusalem, asking, "Where is the child who has been born king of the Jews? For we observed his star in the east and have come to pay him homage." When King Herod heard this, he was frightened, and all Jerusalem with him, and calling together all the chief priests and scribes of the people, he inquired of them where the Messiah was to be born. They told him, "In Bethlehem of Judea, for so it has been written by the prophet:

'And you, Bethlehem, in the land of Judah,
are by no means least among the rulers of Judah,
for from you shall come a ruler
who is to shepherd my people Israel.'"

Then Herod secretly called for the magi and learned from them the exact time when the star had appeared. Then he sent them to Bethlehem, saying, "Go and search diligently for the child, and when you have found him, bring me word so that I may also go and pay him homage." When they had heard the king, they set out, and there, ahead of them, went the star that they had seen in the east, until it stopped over the place where the child was. When they saw that the star had stopped, they were overwhelmed with joy.

On entering the house, they saw the child with Mary his mother, and they knelt down and paid him homage. Then, opening their treasure chests, they offered him gifts of gold, frankincense, and myrrh. And having been warned in a dream not to return to Herod, they left for their own country by another road.

(Matthew 2:1-12)

May the kings of Tarshish and of the isles
render him tribute:
may the kings of Sheba and Seba
bring gifts.
May all kings fall down before him,
all nations give him service.

(Psalm 72:10-11)

I love reading Matthew's story of the wise men's journey, first to Jerusalem, then to Bethlehem, to find and pay homage to the Christ Child, and finally their departure from the scene by heading home by another way. At first glance, it conjures memories of my own children and their participation in church Christmas pageants through the years, dressed in varying colors of house robes, donned with turbans constructed of towels and carrying household objects that could possibly pass for exotic and expensive gifts fit for a king. But as I ponder those many pageants, I recall that this scripture was rarely (if ever) read. Instead, the wise men typically entered stage left after Luke's Gospel story had been read—after Mary and Joseph traveled across the stage during the census of Emperor Augustus to Bethlehem during her pregnancy, after they were seemingly turned away from the inn, after they laid their baby in a manger, and after shepherds (also clothed in house robes) and sweet little angels, dressed in white sheets and gossamer wings, all surrounded the baby Jesus.

The wise men entered not to Scripture but to song that provided a royal backdrop to the evening: "We three kings of Orient are; bearing gifts we traverse afar, field and fountain, moor and mountain, following yonder star."[1] I think the reason we don't typically hear all of this scripture read at children's Christmas pageants is because it is full of mystery and intrigue, and there is, if you listen closely, a sinister air in Herod calling the wise men "secretly" and imploring them to come back and let him know where this king is once they find him. Presumably, he wished to pay him homage as well. You know things are serious when the wise men are warned in a dream not to return to Herod. Intermingled with the excitement, awe, and joy of finding the Christ Child, and the worshipful reverence due him, is also a hint of foreboding darkness and fear. This is something we might want to protect small children from experiencing, but something we, as mature persons of faith, will turn our eyes toward as we follow these wise men on their journey and beyond.

God interrupts the lives of these wise men, just as God interrupted the lives of Mary and Joseph, as they were going about their daily lives. The wise men's journey is upended not once, but twice—by a guiding star and then by a protective dream. Their detours lead them to the Christ Child and home again by another road. Their protective dream is followed by Joseph having one as well, one that more fully reveals Herod's sinister nature and the light, hope, and peace the Christ Child brings into a sometimes dark and turbulent world.

On Bikes, Fires, Taking Detours, and Becoming Neighbors

Have you ever embarked on a planned journey, either an actual one or a life journey, only to find yourself mid trip taking a detour; taking another road, another way of life, or another path? A way that led to new surprises, new friends, or new ways of being? Perhaps you, like me in my call to ministry, found yourself on a path you thought you would always travel in your career only to have it interrupted by God, or others. That interruption may have led you to a totally new and exciting journey. Or perhaps your state of mind or being was interrupted in a way that led you to a new, healthier, or more spiritual way of viewing the world or those around you.

My husband and I spend summers on a mountain in Colorado to escape the brutal Texas heat, and we have discovered we are not alone. Barely a week, if not a day, goes by that we don't meet someone from Texas, and even our home city, Dallas.

One morning, feeling extremely discouraged due to circumstances in our country where I continue to see many of our neighbors being cruelly mistreated due to their racial and national identities, and feeling impotent because I haven't been able to do enough to change those circumstances, I drove up to the summit of the mountain to hike one of my favorite trails. Ever since I was a little girl, being in nature has always been my thin place, the place where I sense the veil between God and earth lifted, where God's presence is unmistakable and palpable. And so, I was trying to clear my head, pray, and hopefully find some answers and a new state of mind on the trail.

Reaching the summit, I turned away from my intentional path toward the trailhead to my left and impulsively turned my car to the right instead to see if I could catch a glimpse in the distance of a wildfire that had been sparked by lightning a few days before. It rained the night before, and I was hoping the fire had been extinguished. Sadly, smoke was still billowing from the direction of fire, so I turned around and headed back toward the trailhead. Not far ahead I saw a young woman sitting on the edge of the road next to her toppled bicycle. At first, she appeared as if she might just be taking a rest (the 9,200-foot climb to the top of the mountain is a steep one), but then I noticed she had blood streaming down one leg, so I pulled over, got out of the car, approached her, and asked if she was okay and if she needed help. She did indeed need help. She explained that she had hit some loose gravel, went headfirst over her handlebars, landed on her shoulder, and feared she had broken her collarbone. Trembling from the excruciating pain of the fall, she asked if I could help her call her husband to let him know what had happened.

As I was tending to her, another car approached, which is unusual at this high point of the mountain. Only committed hikers and cyclists travel up this far, and there aren't many of those. As the car began to pass us, it stopped and a passenger rolled down a window to ask if we needed help. I assured her that I was about to take the young woman home, and they were free to go.

After gingerly helping the injured woman into my car and loading her bike into the cargo space, I began the drive to her nearby home, where her husband was waiting to take her to the hospital. She said, "I'm so glad you came along when you did. I didn't know what I was going to do." And I thought to myself, if I hadn't felt compelled to take that detour to check on the fire first, she wouldn't have fallen yet, and I would have passed by a perfectly content cyclist on a cool mountain morning.

Having delivered the woman into the care of her husband, I drove back to the trail, and as I climbed, I thanked God for giving me the privilege of being able to offer a small act of kindness to someone who was in distress. As I approached the top of the trail with its magnificent vista overlooking the valley below, there was a group of four women taking in the view. One of them yelled down to me, "How is your daughter?" It was the women in the passing car! After clarifying that the woman had been a stranger before our encounter, I gave them a report on her condition. They too said that the injured woman was lucky I came by. I replied, "The truth is, if I hadn't stopped, you certainly would have done so."

I said, "You know, in our world today, we are made to believe that evil lurks around every corner, but the truth is that most people have good hearts and are people like you, eager to offer acts of kindness whenever they can."

We walked along together for a while and they asked if I was from Dallas. They were, and they had noticed a well-known Dallas dealership tag on the back of my car. We were neighbors, yet strangers, who found one another a thousand miles from home.

This path by which strangers become neighbors brings to mind Jesus's teachings in the parable of the good Samaritan in Luke 10:25-37. You may recall that the story begins with an "expert in the law" testing Jesus, asking how to inherit eternal life. Jesus responds with the two greatest commandments: "You shall love the Lord your God with all your heart and with all your soul and with all your strength and with all your mind and your neighbor as yourself" (v. 27). But the expert presses further: "And who is my neighbor?" (v. 29). That is when Jesus tells the parable, and since it is probably the most well-known one in the Gospels, I won't go through the details here. But one of the clear implications of Jesus's teaching here is that "neighbor" doesn't just mean people who live close to us or are similar to us or want the same things we do. A neighbor is anyone we encounter whom we can show God's love to. Living out God's love is how strangers become neighbors.

That day on the mountain, my journey began in discouragement, feeling inadequate for the massive task of caring for those I see who have been dehumanized, mistreated, and marginalized—those whom I see as my neighbors. So I sought connection with God. I found it, but not in the way I intended and expected. It was the detour, that unexpected interruption, that led me back to God and gave me an opportunity to show God's love to someone in need. Like the magi, and later Joseph as well, I came home by a way I hadn't planned. And that detour gave me the opportunity to offer love, help, and protection to a neighbor in need. It is often in those moments, moments where we offer God's love to others, that we ourselves draw closest to God.

On the Magi Becoming Neighbors

The wise men mentioned in the scripture above are mysterious travelers on a journey that seems odd to us in today's world, perhaps odd even to those living in Jesus's day. Their narrative rates high on the list of Christmas stories in its ability to capture the imagination. That is, we don't know much about them, so it's easy to fill in the gaps in our knowledge with a variety of images and ideas.

For starters, in most Bible translations they are called "wise men" or "magi," the latter originating from the Greek word used in Matthew, *magos*. They have also variously been represented as astrologers, magicians, Persian priests, or a combination of all of the above. So there's some confusion as to what we should even call them. We are even at a loss as to their country of origin. We know only that they come "from the east" (Matthew 2:1). More likely than not, they hailed from Persia or Babylonia, though others have also included India and Arabia as possibilities. Lore has placed in our minds that there were three wise men, probably due to the number of gifts they laid before the baby. Manuscripts penned as early as the sixth century had given the wise men names. However, William Wadsworth Longfellow, in his then-popular poem "The Three Kings," forever sealed in our contemporary memory the names Melchior, Gaspar, and Balthasar.[2] Even since the third century many referred to the magi as kings because of prophetic scriptures indicating kings would bow down and worship the king of Israel, and all nations would serve him (Psalm 72:10-11).

What's most important isn't knowing exactly where the wise men were from, how many there were, or if they were kings, priests, or astrologers (though I'm partial to astrologers since they *did* read the stars to find Jesus). It's more important, at least for the author of Matthew, for us to see these mysterious travelers from the east as symbolic of the world coming to understand who Jesus is and revere him. Herod does not understand his significance, but these three men from a far-off land traveled many miles to meet this newborn king. They know there is something special about Jesus and are welcomed in to see him and his family.

As we saw in the last chapter, Matthew introduces Jesus as the descendant of foreign "others"—people who were probably not naturally seen as part of Christ's story. In the same vein, the wise men remind us that God has always and will always include the other in God's story of love, redemption, and new creation. They remind us that we are all neighbors, all God's children, in search of God's love, and we are all welcomed into God's presence. As a matter of fact, God, like the eager father in the parable of the prodigal son, does more than welcome us into his presence; God runs to meet us with arms open wide (Luke 15:11-32). This Advent season, as we wait for the coming of the Christ Child, we can know that God eagerly waits for us and welcomes us and all of our neighbors.

An Upended Journey

Chapter 2 of Matthew's account of the wise men's journey begins, "In the time of King Herod, after Jesus was born in

Bethlehem of Judea. . . ." (v. 1). We aren't told how Mary and Joseph make their way to Bethlehem. Matthew doesn't mention the census we find in Luke. If you had never read Luke's account of Jesus's birth, you might assume that Mary and Joseph had always lived in Bethlehem, not Nazareth, for the wise men come to a house in Bethlehem, not a manger (Matthew 2:11). However, both Matthew and Luke agree that Jesus was born in Bethlehem during the reign of King Herod the Great.

It is at this moment in history that wise men, perhaps astrologers, from the east seemed to have witnessed something extraordinary as they studied stars in the night sky. I sense that stargazing was their "thin place," just as being in nature is mine. Apparently, not only were the magi familiar with the significance of the constellations, but also they must have learned of some Hebrew Scriptures predicting the birth of a Davidic king. They had studied the stars for years when they noticed either a confluence of planets, or an alignment of certain stars that indicated to them that a king, *this king*, had been born. Their day-to-day lives were interrupted, divinely upended, upon seeing this sign. In their estimation, this astrological event was so astounding that this new king had to be found. They were drawn to go and pay him homage.

Often translated as "homage," the Greek word *proskuneo* means to physically bow down, or prostrate oneself in order to show reverence. It comes from the two words *pros* (meaning "toward") and *kuneo* (meaning "to kiss"). It refers to the act of showing reverence or worship and can include the physical act of prostrating oneself or bowing. As we've already discussed, these magi are symbolic of Jesus's inclusion of and reach into all the nations of the world. God told Abraham that he would be blessed to be a blessing to all the nations of the world (Genesis 12:1-3). The family that would rise from him was to live as an example of God's love, mercy, and justice in order that all the nations would be drawn to God.

And yet, during Jesus's day, while Gentile "God-fearers" were welcomed to worship, pray, and study at the temple in the Court of the Gentiles, the outermost courtyard of the temple, they were not allowed to cross into the more sacred inner courts. In fact, inscriptions were posted warning of severe consequences, even death, for Gentiles who proceeded past a certain point. In the magi, or wise men, Matthew foresees how those outside the Jewish community would come to understand who Jesus is.

Lest we begin to feel smug and think that we as Christians would never have turned away others from worship, we need not travel far back in history, or even the last decade or two, to see that humanity still likes to create outsiders and divisions, even in the church. During the Civil War, Black and White people worshipped together in some churches, but in segregated areas. Additionally, Black people were never allowed leadership positions and were required to give up their seats for a White person. Some enslaved people were allowed to have their own Sunday meetings, but normally under close supervision.

There is also a widely known story about Ghandi, who was Hindu, being rejected from entering a church in Calcutta. The story goes that Ghandi had read the Gospels, was intrigued by Jesus's teachings, and was interested in perhaps becoming a Christian. One Sunday morning he stopped by a church but was turned away because he was neither from a high caste nor White.

This experience helped shape a quotation often attributed to him: "If it weren't for Christians, I'd be a Christian."

Today, segregation of sorts still exists in churches. There are still many churches where either women or LGBTQ+ persons, or both, are not allowed to be involved in pastoral or leadership roles. Although not intentionally, many churches exclude the elderly or those with cognitive and physical disabilities from being able to fully participate in worship or other activities. This led our church many years ago to offer shuttle buses to drive our more senior congregants to church from their assisted living homes. We also keep wheelchairs at all of the entrances to the church and staff volunteers to help people to their classes and worship spaces. Additionally, we started a ministry for those with cognitive and physical disabilities. Our disabled neighbors now have their own worship service, Sunday morning classes, and the chance to participate each year in Spotlight Theatre, a play created by and for the disability community to allow those who are normally excluded from such opportunities to be the stars of the show.

All this is to say that we, too, can be insular in the way we plan and approach worship, and in the way we want to set boundaries around who is and is not worthy to approach God. But the magi and Jesus call us to travel another way, to truly come home to God by a better path.

I imagine the wise men heading out on their long journey, following the direction in which they had seen this astrological sign, this star of wonder, with determination and excitement. In order to discover where the new king had been born, it would make sense to start their search in Jerusalem. After all, that is where the current king of the region lived. When they arrive in Jerusalem, they assume everyone would already know about this new king, so they begin asking, "Where is the child who has been born king of the Jews? For we observed his star and have come to pay him homage" (Matthew 2:2). They are eager to find this new king and believe everyone in Jerusalem will be as excited as they are about his birth. Instead, Scripture tells us that the birth of "the king of the Jews" is news to Herod and all of Jerusalem. And the news is frightening to *everyone*. Why would the Jewish leadership be afraid of a new king? Could they perhaps feel threatened by the possibility?

Herod was not a Davidic king. He was thought by many of his subjects to be an illegitimate king because his family had converted to Judaism, he was not from a ruling dynasty, and he had been appointed by the Roman senate to rule over Judea. In other words, he was beholden to the Roman Empire for his kingship—and for his power. Maintaining his position required that he keep Rome happy at all costs. Herod was also despotic in his attempts to remain in power. Numerous citizens of Herod had been killed by him due to his paranoia that they were plotting against him. In addition, his wife, her two sons, her brother, her grandfather, and her mother were murdered for the same reason. Of course Herod is frightened! But why was all of Jerusalem with him? Perhaps they knew that there might be trouble for everyone when the violent Herod (who reportedly ordered many people in Jerusalem to be murdered upon his death in order to incite an appropriate level of mourning) discovers there is an authentic

Davidic king in Israel. There would be crackdowns, curfews, roundups of suspected enemies, and more Roman troops with their swords and spears marching through the city. If a regime change were to occur, the religious leadership could possibly lose their jobs, or worse. This child, it seems, is perceived as a potential political threat. Thus, the news of the Messiah's birth is met not with jubilation but with fear. Or as theologian Thomas G. Long states, "The birth of the Messiah undermines all pretenders to the throne. Indeed, the gospel . . . threatens all who would dominate others. Whenever the true nature of the gospel is understood by the powers-that-be, all swaggering despots turn fearful."[3]

The Metropolitan Museum of Art in New York City displays a Nativity scene each year during the Christmas season that incorporates all of the familiar subjects: Mary, Joseph, baby Jesus, shepherds, cattle, wise men, and angels. What is striking, however, is that scene is set not in a stable in Bethlehem but within the toppled and crumbled columns of a once magnificent Roman building. The theological implication of this scene is clear enough. While the birth of the Messiah is a humble one, his entry into the world shakes its very foundations, announcing, as Mary did in the Magnificat, the fall of the proud and mighty, and those who wish to cling to power. Jesus's way of love is always a threat to the ways of oppression in all forms.

And this brings me back to one of our baptismal vows I quoted earlier: "Do you accept the freedom and power God gives you to resist, evil, injustice, and oppression in whatever forms they may present themselves?"[4] Part of Jesus's mission on this earth was to dismantle injustice through love of God and neighbor. There is a quote widely attributed to Dietrich Bonhoeffer, a German minister during World War II, who was imprisoned and killed for his resistance against Hitler and his regime, that says, "We are not to simply bandage the wounds of victims beneath the wheels of injustice; we are to drive a spoke into the wheel itself." Despots like Hitler and Herod are to be resisted. Any actions that create hardship and suffering for others are to be resisted. And we offer that resistance through love.

When Herod discovers the wise men are looking to find a new king of the Jews, he summons the brightest biblical scholars in Jerusalem: all of the chief priests (those responsible for services and administration of the temple, among other important functions) and scribes (the interpreters of Jewish law and traditions). He asks them where the Messiah was to be born. Their answer:

> *In Bethlehem of Judea, for so it has been written by the prophet:*
>
> *"And you, Bethlehem, in the land of Judah,*
> *are by no means least among the rulers of Judah,*
> *for from you shall come a ruler*
> *who is to shepherd my people Israel."*
>
> *(Matthew 2:5-6)*

The chief priests' and scribes' response that the child shall be born in Bethlehem (David's birthplace) comes from Micah 5:2. That he will "shepherd my people Israel" suggests numerous biblical resonances, perhaps especially with the Messiah's shepherding the people as King David had (2 Samuel 5:2). Throughout the Old Testament, God often refers to the leaders of Israel, both kings and religious leaders, as shepherds. Two of

Israel's greatest leaders had been actual shepherds. Moses, who led Israel out of slavery in Egypt, had been tending his sheep on Mount Sinai when he heard God's voice calling him from a burning bush to lead his people out of slavery and the oppression of Pharaoh (Exodus 3:1-10). The unassuming shepherd boy David, the youngest son of Jesse, had been summoned from the fields as he was tending his sheep to come into his father's house. The prophet Samuel had been sent by God to Jesse's house in Bethlehem to anoint a new king from among Jesse's sons. They had all, except for the youngest, lined up for Samuel, but God rejected each of them. When David made his way into the house, with the smell of the field and sheep still lingering on his hair and clothes, God tells Samuel, "Rise and anoint him, for this is the one" (1 Samuel 16:12b). David had been a good shepherd of the people of Israel. From Bethlehem, once again, would come another good shepherd.

The wise men, it seems, know at least something about Judaism or the Hebrew Scriptures, as they arrive in Jerusalem asking, "Where is the child who has been born king of the Jews?" (Matthew 2:2). Coming from a different cultural and religious background (the magi are often speculated to be followers of Zoroastrianism, an ancient Persian religion), they might not know much, but they must have had powerful experience seeing that star—powerful enough to prod them to undertake a long and potentially dangerous journey to see the newborn Jesus. Perhaps without even knowing it or fully understanding why and how, they heard the voice of God calling to them, telling them that something momentous was happening and that they should just go and see for themselves.

The magi followed their guiding star the last five miles of their journey to Bethlehem, and when it stopped, they were "overwhelmed with joy" (Matthew 2:10). They had been anticipating this moment for quite some time. When they enter the Holy Family's home, notice what the scripture says came first—not the gifts but a show of respect and reverence. "On entering the house, they saw the child with Mary his mother, and they knelt down and paid him homage" (v. 11a). Those who were outsiders to the faith, both ethnically and theologically, have come to understand something about his importance. As such, they lower themselves before him. "Then [and only then!], opening their treasure chests, they offered him gifts of gold, frankincense, and myrrh" (v. 11b). First, they kneel, then they offer gifts.

When has your heart been so overwhelmed with joy that your first response was to bow down and worship or give thanks to God? Perhaps at seeing your own child immediately after their birth? I know that was the case for me. But it also happened during my wedding to my husband. The pastor who conducted the service was wise enough to have my husband and me kneel after our vows were made. Then he prayed over us a blessing, and we recited together, for the first time as husband and wife, the Lord's Prayer. Reciting our vows was one of the most joyful moments of my life. And I was glad that, immediately after, we could pay homage to the One who had brought us to that moment.

The story of the magi comes to an end with their experiencing a dream of warning. God spoke to Joseph, the son of David, through a dream, and now God speaks to these Gentiles, who are sons of a different family, in the same way. Although no angel is present in their dream, there is no doubt that the warning is divine in origin. Their obedient response to God's voice frustrates Herod's plot to kill the Christ Child. They will not return to Jerusalem. They will not play a role in Herod's evil power play. Through their action, they will drive a spoke in the wheel of injustice that this evil shepherd of Israel has designed. The King of kings, the rising Good Shepherd is safe for now.

As we watch them fade into the distance, this will be the last time we see the magi, but their significance in Matthew's story, the story of Jesus, will continue to beckon us to go home by another path. We will recall their journey at the end of Matthew, when the disciples meet the resurrected Christ in Galilee: "When they saw him, they worshiped him" (Matthew 28:17). Then Jesus tells them, "Go therefore and make disciples of all nations" (Matthew 28:19). At Jesus's birth, these Gentile visitors journey to a far-off land in order to worship the king of the Jews. At the end of Matthew, the movement runs in reverse, the message moving out into the wider world for all to see. Now we, as disciples of Christ, are called to journey from our places of worship to invite all of our neighbors in. We are called to serve our neighbors who are in need and might be different from us but who are also children of the God of the universe.

I began this chapter with the story of my becoming neighbors with strangers through following a path of service that God laid out. My journey began with discouragement over the mistreatment of neighbors in our country, mistreatment that creates darkness in their lives and in our world. The wise men, former outsiders who now share a point of connection with Christians as they seek out and revere Jesus, were strangers who became neighbors to Jesus and his family. They teach us a great lesson in what it means to be diligent in searching after the newborn king, being open to God's divine guidance in following an unexpected life path, recognizing the importance of Scripture in confirming that path, and keeping our hearts open to serving and embracing outsiders as neighbors in our midst.

Today, if you are discouraged and feel as if you aren't able to do enough to change the circumstances in the world around you, if you feel as if the Herods of the world seem to have the upper hand, know that you can go home by another way. You can begin your new journey by showing the love of God to your nearest neighbor in need of comfort, acceptance, and love. Follow the star of the wise men, listen to the voice that calls you to a new path and a new way of being.

THE SHEPHERDS

The Surprise of Joy

CHAPTER 4

CHAPTER 4

The Shepherds

The Surprise of Joy

Now in that same region there were shepherds living in the fields, keeping watch over their flock by night. Then an angel of the Lord stood before them, and the glory of the Lord shone around them, and they were terrified. But the angel said to them, "Do not be afraid, for see, I am bringing you good news of great joy for all the people: to you is born this day in the city of David a Savior, who is the Messiah, the Lord. This will be a sign for you: you will find a child wrapped in bands of cloth and lying in a manger." And suddenly there was with the angel a multitude of the heavenly host, praising God and saying,

> *"Glory to God in the highest heaven,*
> *and on earth peace among those whom he favors!"*

When the angels had left them and gone into heaven, the shepherds said to one another, "Let us go now to Bethlehem and see this thing that has taken place, which the Lord has made known to us." So they went with haste and found Mary and Joseph and the child lying in the manger. When they saw this, they made known what had been told them about this child, and all who heard it were amazed at what the shepherds told them, and Mary treasured all these words and pondered them in her heart. The shepherds returned, glorifying and praising God for all they had heard and seen, as it had been told them.

(Luke 2:8-20)

As Luke's Christmas story comes to an end, the narrative shifts away from those who had direct contact with angels foretelling the miraculous births of their children, who are destined for greatness in God's eyes. That shift introduces us to the people who will be the first hearers of the good news that a Savior has been born in the city of David. Will this news first be heralded to the king in Jerusalem by royal criers? Will news of the birth be announced at the gates of the temple for all of the devout religious leaders to hear? The answer is a surprising and resounding no. Those who are privileged to hear the first announcement of the birth of the Messiah are not who we in today's world, or those of Jesus's day, would expect. They are not well-known political leaders. They have no standing in the religious circles of the temple. Indeed, they don't even have any particular social standing. The angels who herald the "good news of great joy for all the people" (Luke 2:10) do so not at a palace or the temple. Instead, they approach the first recipients of this good news where they work and live: in the fields, in the darkness of night.

For Luke, and for Mary in the Magnificat, this detail is quite significant. While Matthew impresses upon us that Jesus is born through the royal lineage of David, and that Gentile "kings" came from afar to pay him homage, Luke has another very important point to make. Luke, you may recall, keeps front and center the message that Jesus has come to bring good news to the poor, the oppressed, the sick, the downtrodden, the powerless, and the hopeless. So it is fitting that angels, God's messengers, first herald this good news of great joy to the most unassuming people in society: shepherds. God's lifting up of the lowly began in this story, with the childless Elizabeth and favored peasant girl Mary, and it continues now with the shepherds. These humble field workers, whose main job had been the care of sheep, will now be the first ones to hear the multitude of heavenly angels declare, "Glory to God in the highest heaven, / and on earth peace among those whom he favors!" (Luke 2:14). Indeed, not only are they first to hear the good news, the shepherds are also the first charged with the holy privilege of sharing these extraordinary and glad tidings with others. The lowly and humble shepherds will be lifted to the status of the first evangelists in Luke's Gospel.

Joy Breaks in Where We Least Expect It

My husband and I met when we were both a little older. I had come to a point in life where I was quite content being single and wished never again to be set up on another date. Blind dates then were much like meeting someone on a dating app today, only worse. At least on a dating app you get to look at some profiles and choose the person with whom you will have the date rather than relying on friends who say things like, "Whenever I see him, I think of you, and how perfect you would be together." Then you're left wondering after the date, "How in the world did my friend think this person and I could *ever* be compatible?" After *many* years of less-than-ideal blind dates, I made a vow to myself:

absolutely no more blind dates. Nada. None. Zero. The vow held until a friend called one day to say she knew someone whom I must meet. She asked, "Can I give Ike your number?" I told her I had sworn off blind dates. "But this really won't be like a blind date. It's just a Memorial Day party at our house. You could meet him here and be on your way. Come on! He's a lot of fun, and I think you'll like him." Reluctantly, I agreed.

Ike called the next day asking what time he could pick me up for the pool party. "Oh, that won't be necessary. I'll just meet you there."

"No really," he said, "I insist."

I dug in, "I really do live out of the way, and it would be much easier if I just meet you there."

Ike persisted, "My mother raised me to have good manners, and she would be horrified if she knew I made a date with someone and didn't pick them up."

In my mind, this wasn't a date, but I relented, "I'll see you at noon at my place on Monday then."

On our first Memorial Day "date," I was reserved, asking questions but not speaking much. Afterward, I thought, *This man seems so nice, and I was a dud date. I will probably never hear from him again.* But the next week Ike called. We went out to dinner and talked for hours. His transparency, honesty, character, and integrity (and good manners) came shining through, and for the first time in many years, I thought I had met someone who could possibly be a good life partner. When I least expected it, I was surprised by joy. The joy of meeting someone with the same values and interests I held. The joy of an easy relationship with no drama and little friction. We were married two years later—on Memorial Day weekend.

Since we were "a little older," we hoped to have children as quickly as possible but knew that time, and age, was not particularly on our side. However, I soon found myself being plagued with fatigue and falling asleep at my computer at work. I also had the sudden urge to drink chocolate milk and eat Milano cookies (things I had never done before). Finally alert to the subtle signs, I stopped at a drug store on my way to work one morning. When I deposited Milano cookies, chocolate milk, and a pregnancy test on the check-out station, the clerk, a wise, middle-aged woman, smiled at me and said, "I bet it's positive." She was right.

Indescribable joy broke into our lives, yet again, when we least expected it. And by our first Christmas season as a married couple, we were experiencing awe and wonder, we were certain, that was as strong as Mary and Joseph's over their own soon-to-be born child.

Being pregnant during the Christmas season has a way of bringing home the wonder of new life, of being a co-agent in creation with God. It illumines more deeply the sacredness of the season. It makes it easier to imagine Mary and Joseph's unbelievable joy, but also their natural concerns about the well-being of their baby. I guess I had never thought that Mary and Joseph might have worried about certain things—until I did. Will we be good parents? How will I know what to do? How do we best provide for this child? Do I need to work more to make money or less so I can give my time and attention? What will our future hold? How can I prepare my child for it? Mary and Joseph may not have had our identical concerns, but they were no doubt similar. Yet, in the midst of those concerns was incredible joy in knowing that God had led them to this moment in their lives and in their life with this precious child. We felt the same.

The week of Christmas that year found me on doctor-ordered bedrest. Along with the natural worry for the baby's welfare also came an unnatural, God-given sense of peace and joy in the midst of that concern. We had already, in our unbridled joy, purchased the kind of gifts we hoped we could give one day to our child for other children. We presented these treasures to the local mall's Angel Tree as reverently as magi bearing gifts of gold, frankincense, and myrrh. We lavished on these children what we wished every child could receive at Christmas: a bicycle, basketball, roller skates, dolls, and other things I can't even remember. We hoped these children would know that they were as loved and special as all children of God. We wanted to share with a child we would never know the love we would soon share with our own baby. Joy also bubbled up unexpectedly in the midst of our giving. The joy that was there only grew as we gave it away.

Joy has a way of doing that, of breaking in when we least expect it. Sometimes it breaks in with the joy that you longed and hoped for but had grown weary in the waiting or given up on expecting—like meeting the person you want to spend the rest of your life with, or becoming pregnant against great odds. Joy also has a way of breaking in even during moments of grief or crisis. It doesn't replace the grief or make the crisis go away, but it reminds us that even in the midst of trying times, there is still goodness, love, and light. God's presence, grace, and goodness still abound in times of difficulty, offering us hope for the days ahead.

This past summer, in the dark early morning hours of July 4, 2025, a massive flood hit the Texas Hill Country. Calm streams and rivers immediately became deathly torrents. The Guadalupe River rose a devastating twenty-six feet in just forty-five minutes, ravaging an area in Hunt, Texas, where numerous summer camps dot the river's edge. In a matter of minutes these renowned havens of carefree childhood memories and summer's delights became filled with the horror of rising, rushing water, sweeping away entire cabins. Twenty-seven young girls and counselors from Camp Mystic, the camp that was hardest hit, perished in the floods. Six of those girls were from Highland Park, a small township nestled within the heart of the large city of Dallas, where my home church is located. Two of those children's families attend our church. The entirety of Dallas, and Texas, was overcome with grief at the unfathomable and tragic loss experienced by all 135 families whose loved ones perished in the flood, but the deaths of those six children hit home. The numbers were no longer just statistics; they were children we knew. Their mothers, fathers, sisters, brothers, aunts, uncles, and grandparents were all people we knew and loved.

By the next morning, mobilization of first responders, churches, volunteer organizations, and just individuals who cared deeply had already begun. Search and rescue teams came from all over the US. Restaurant owners made their way to the Hill Country to feed those in need. Green ribbons (the camp's signature color) were tied on just about every tree in Dallas exhibiting every person's love and care for the girls who were missing, as a sign to their families that they were loved, supported, and not forgotten. Most of those ribbons still remain months later.

Stories of heroism and faith also began to emerge. One such story came from a camp counselor who had sixteen young girls in her and two other counselors' care. She awoke to hear water coming inside their cabin. When her feet hit the floor, water was already covering her ankles. She and her fellow counselors began passing children through the windows to get them out of their swiftly flooding cabin as rapids began encircling them and water rose above the counselors' knees. Carrying and holding on to the children, they began running uphill. Water began to overtake them, but they kept moving up. Once they reached higher ground, they sat in the rain together and prayed throughout the treacherous night.[1] Although sunrise brought devastating news of tremendous loss, there was also great joy in knowing 167 were saved from the floodwaters.

The week of July 4, two friends were visiting us in Colorado. We woke that morning to the news of what had happened overnight. One of the friends had attended Camp Mystic as a child. She and her daughters had all attended, and all had been camp counselors. They intimately knew some of those who had perished in the flood. During the day, we prayed for the families who had learned of the loss of their children, and for the camp director, who lost his life trying to save children. We also rejoiced with every story of survival and rescue.

Again, joy doesn't replace our grief or make the crisis go away, but it reminds us that even in the midst of our trying times, there is still goodness, love, and light. God's presence, grace, and goodness still abound in times of difficulty, offering us hope for the days ahead. It's the reason we can laugh as we tell stories of a loved one who has died. We grieve their loss but can still take great joy in their life and the sweet moments we shared with them. We can even experience joy in knowing that they are eternally held in God's arms.

I have a friend who, like most all of us, was affected by the COVID-19 pandemic. Her family was cut off from their usual support systems for a time. Her daughter's graduation was canceled. Then her husband lost his job. The family's circumstances looked bleak. However, as we began talking about joy surprisingly breaking into our lives when we least expect it, she said, "We look back on those perpetual snow days, with our family huddled outside telling stories, playing games, with laughter filling the air, and we realize that we experienced so much joy even in the midst of all this darkness. We found a great deal of blessing in our circumstances." Thanks be to God that joy breaks in when we least expect it.

The Joy of the Shepherds

Imagine, for a moment, being the shepherds in Luke's Gospel. They are doing what they do every day and every night: keeping close watch over their precious animals. They lead their sheep to the best grazing areas by day. At night, they protect the flock from predators by gathering them into a stone-walled sheep fold, cave, or temporary handmade structure. The entrance of the enclosures would be covered by thorny brush or the shepherds' own bodies lying across it as protection for the sheep. While we may imagine sheep wandering loose in large fields while the shepherds watch over them by night, they were more than likely in an enclosed area, with the shepherds keeping watch over them.

Luke tells us, "In that same region there were shepherds living in the fields, keeping watch over their flock by night." (Luke 2:8). Notice here that it is night. The shepherds are in the darkness of night, which reflects the prophetic words Zechariah speaks when his miraculously conceived son, John the Baptist, is born to Elizabeth:

Because of the tender mercy of our God,
the dawn from on high will break upon us,
to shine upon those who sit in darkness and in the shadow of death,
to guide our feet into the way of peace.
(Luke 1:78-79)

Zechariah's words loosely quote Isaiah 9:2, 6:

The people who walked in darkness
have seen a great light;
those who lived in a land of deep darkness—
on them light has shined. . . .
For a child has been born for us,
a son given to us;
authority rests upon his shoulders;
and he is named
Wonderful Counselor, Mighty God,
Everlasting Father, Prince of Peace.

Of course, this familiar prophetic scripture is read each year during the Advent season. It is one that continually fills us with joy, hope, and peace.

The angel's visitation breaks into the literal darkness of the shepherds' lives, and symbolically into the lives of all who live in the darkness of marginalization and oppression, who carry the burdensome yoke of being seen as less than or not good enough, of being underpaid and undervalued, of living in fear of the ever-present Roman sword and spear. The angel of the Lord "stood before them, and the glory of the Lord shone around them, and they were terrified" (Luke 2:9). The darkness of the entire night sky is ablaze with the angel's presence, with the glory of the Lord. The glory of God washes over everything, including the shepherds. God's glory is often discussed as revealing itself as light (Isaiah 60:1; Luke 2:9; Revelation 21:11). With the angel's appearance and pronouncement of the good news, the light shining on those who live in darkness has come. And the shepherds, rightfully so, are terrified! I love the King James Version, which expresses the shepherds fear quite like none other: "and they were sore afraid" (Luke 2:9). In response to their being sore afraid, the angel says to them:

> *"Do not be afraid, for see, I am bringing you good news of great joy for all the people: to you is born this day in the city of David a Savior, who is the Messiah, the Lord. This will be a sign for you: you will find a child wrapped in bands of cloth and lying in a manger." And suddenly there was with the angel a multitude of the heavenly host, praising God and saying,*
>
> *"Glory to God in the highest heaven,*
> *and on earth peace among those whom he favors!"*
>
> *(Luke 2:10-14)*

To *you* is born this day. This newborn Messiah is born *to them*. This is good news of great joy for *them*, that will soon spread into the world. This baby has come to bring light, joy, and peace to *them* personally, *and* to all others. The angel wants them to know that they will not be left out of the blessings this promised Savior brings. Once the angel shares this incredible news, the sky is filled not only with the awe-inspiring glory and light of the Lord; it is also filled with the heavenly host as well, proclaiming the glory and peace of God. This is not peace procured at the end of a Roman spear or by some other threat of force. Rather, this is the true peace that can only be found in the righteousness and justice that come from the deep love of God.

To *you* is born this day—yes, *you*. Today. When I was younger, I used to wonder why we spent so much time talking during Advent about waiting for Christ to be born when it was obvious he had already been born. As a more mature person, and pastor, I realize, yes, Christ has been born, but daily I need to realize he was born to and for *me*. He was born for me, lived for me, died for me, and was raised for me—and *you*—and our *neighbor*. And each day I need to remember that birth and allow myself to remain open to his being born in me, yet again.

These words make me think of Jesus being born to Mary, and Mary being the Christ-bearer. If Christ is born to us, to *you*, then you, too, are a Christ-bearer. To *you* is born this day. To *you* who may feel less than, not good enough, overlooked, or sidelined. To *you* who may be, for this season, living in a land of deep darkness—the darkness of grief, rejection, depression, anxiety, abuse, addiction, or marginalization of any kind—on *you*, light has shined. To *you* has been born a Savior, who is the Messiah.

We live in terrifying times. Times when we, too, are sore afraid. Most times in history have had terrifying moments. Most times in history have had Herods bent on ruling through keeping people afraid, terrified either of losing their own power or of the "other," or through ginning up irrational fears in the hearts of their subjects. Authoritarian regimes have long known that fear and grievance are effective motivators and stoke them in citizens in order to legitimize their control. And they often seek to control media narratives and communication in order to accomplish this. For example, Hitler was adept at first of making his people afraid of the Jews, the disabled, and of their own neighbors. He then made them all fear him as he controlled the narrative of fear through the media. Jesus's birth announced to the shepherds tells us we no longer need to be afraid. We need not fear those who try to make us fear our neighbors. We need not fear the dark circumstances in our lives. We need to keep our eyes open in the darkness for God's glorious light. We need not be terrified of, or blinded by, the darkness, for on *you* light has shined in the form of a Savior.

This Savior's birth and life show that God through Christ is with us, no matter our circumstances. The circumstances of Jesus's birth, and the way he lived his life, make clear that no one in God's eyes is less than, for it is to those he showed the most compassion and love. For those who feel as if they are already living in the light, and that light is warm and glowing all around, there is a call to share that light with those who are living in darkness. That is how God's justice, mercy, peace, and joy spread.

Sometimes sharing that light is as simple as reaching out to someone who is experiencing loneliness or grief by sending them a card or taking them to coffee or lunch. Sometimes it only involves offering a word of encouragement. Sharing the light could be dropping off a meal for someone just home from the hospital, or it could mean serving people at your local homeless shelter. Sharing the light could also mean shining a light on an injustice you see happening in your community or in the world.

I mentioned earlier that I am part of an interfaith clergy group that prays each week at Immigration and Customs Enforcement headquarters here in Dallas for immigrants who are coming in for their regular interview appointments (they are the ones who are doing things the "right way"). This building is not a detention facility. It is meant only for interviews or processing those who are about to be detained or deported. By law, people can only be held in this facility for twenty-four to forty-eight hours. When our group discovered that people were being detained in this facility for more than a week, having to sleep on the floor with thirty people to a room, with no beds, cots, chairs, air conditioning, or showers, we shined a light on these unjust actions by apprising our local news outlets, our city leaders, and members of Congress of the situation. Sharing the light can also mean shining a light on an injustice you see in the world around you.

During Advent, church services often include this reading from Isaiah 9:2-7. As you read these words, consider how the birth of Jesus might realize this prophetic message:

The people who walked in darkness
have seen a great light;

those who lived in a land of deep darkness—
on them light has shined.
You have multiplied exultation;
you have increased its joy;
they rejoice before you
as with joy at the harvest,
as people exult when dividing plunder.
For the yoke of their burden
and the bar across their shoulders,
the rod of their oppressor,
you have broken as on the day of Midian.
For all the boots of the tramping warriors
and all the garments rolled in blood
shall be burned as fuel for the fire.
For a child has been born for us,
a son given to us;
authority rests upon his shoulders,
and he is named
Wonderful Counselor, Mighty God,
Everlasting Father, Prince of Peace.
Great will be his authority,
and there shall be endless peace
for the throne of David and his kingdom.
He will establish and uphold it
with justice and with righteousness
from this time onward and forevermore.
The zeal of the LORD of hosts will do this.

As we read these words, there are still wars around the globe—some that have lasted for years. Herods are still among us. Boots of trampling warriors are still among us. Many still live under the yoke and burden of oppression in this country, and around the world. So how do we exult at this reading during Advent? What does it mean that these unrighteous actions will not exist with the coming of the Messiah?

We read these words during Advent with great hope and anticipation that someday they will all come true. We live between the "already" and the "not yet." We live in the "already" of Jesus's birth, life, death, and resurrection. His life and deeds provide an example of what life could look like if everyone lived and walked the way of Jesus. We live in the "already" of Jesus's followers who are committed to living in the way of Jesus. We live in the "already" of having compassion for those who are hungry, thirsty, imprisoned, sick, strangers, and in need of clothing or shelter (Matthew 25:31-46); for the poor, the captive, the blind, and the oppressed (Luke 4:18-19). Jesus has harsh words for those who say they follow him, but don't actually follow in his way of acting out of compassion for the least of these (Matthew 25:41-46).

And this is the rub, but it's also the great hope. It's why we keep attending Advent and Christmas Eve services. It's why we plead as we sing "O Come, O Come, Emmanuel" and "Come, Thou Long Expected Jesus" each Advent season, and why we exult at his birth with "Joy to the World" on Christmas Eve. We know the more we live like Jesus, the more light we shine and the more darkness is expelled. The more darkness is expelled, the more the world comes to look like the kingdom of God on earth as it is in heaven. The world then comes closer to resembling Isaiah's prophecy. We are "not yet" living into the fulfillment of God's kingdom come on earth; but until Christ returns, we are called to live as fully as we can into the "already." We are called to do so, not only as individuals, but as communities, and communities of faith.

When have you as an individual felt light shine on your darkness by the actions of another person or group of people? How have you been a light to others? How do you see your church community, or other churches or organizations, living into Isaiah's prophetic words and Jesus's words in Matthew 25:40 and 25:45: "Just as you did it to one of the least of these brothers and sisters of mine, you did it to me," and likewise, "Just as you did not do it to one of the least of these, you did not do it to me"?

In some ways, Isaiah's and Jesus's words are already being fulfilled among us, and for that we rejoice. But we also know that many people experience the "not yet" of being adequately fed, employed, housed, released from the chains of oppression, and accepted and welcomed by the world. So we have hope for the day when everyone will experience and know that a great light has shined on them too, and we do what we can in our "already" moments to keep that light shining.

Light has shined on the shepherds watching over their flock by night, and in their unexpected and incredible joy, they announce, "Let us go now to Bethlehem and see this thing that has taken place, which the Lord has made known to us" (Luke 2:15).

The Joy of Mary and Joseph

Mary and Joseph also experience unexpected joy breaking into their lives. Unexpected because it's not difficult to imagine that Mary and Joseph's dream of having their baby in Nazareth was dashed at the prospect of traveling to Bethlehem at the decree of Emperor Augustus. Joseph is required to go to his hometown to register in a census, which, of course, will be the basis for assessing future Roman taxes—taxes that place a heavy burden on everyone living in Judea so that Rome can maintain its massive infrastructure and feed its hungry and ever-growing war machine.

This young couple had, no doubt, anticipated having a local midwife (perhaps the same one who delivered both of them) aid Mary in Jesus's birth. They probably also expected to be surrounded by a host of supportive family and friends. Mothers and grandmothers would be near them to offer loving advice on how to care for Jesus. Friends would pop in to offer congratulations and gush over their beautiful baby boy. But it was not to be.

Mary and Joseph strike out on their ninety-mile journey to Bethlehem, most likely on foot. However, if they were fortunate enough, they may have had a donkey for Mary to ride in her uncomfortable state. The arduous trip would have taken at least seven days, possibly closer to ten. As they approached Jerusalem, just six miles to the north of Bethlehem, the terrain would have been mostly uphill (which is why scriptures always tell us that people are going "up" to Jerusalem—the city rests on a plateau in the Judean Mountains). This would have been a difficult journey, to say the least, for a woman in her last days of pregnancy. Along the way, Mary and Joseph probably worried about the conditions they would face when they arrived in Bethlehem. The entire city would be crowded with visitors arriving for the census. Where would they stay? Would they be able to find a midwife to help with their baby's delivery if the time came while they were there? Or would her body allow her to make the trip back to Nazareth so she could deliver this baby in the perfect setting, surrounded by the people who loved and cared for her most?

Of course, we know, as Luke tells us, that their hopes would be dashed: "While they were there, the time came for her to deliver her child. And she gave birth to her firstborn son and wrapped him in bands of cloth and laid him in a manger, because there was no place in the guest room" (Luke 2:6-7).

As much as our Hallmark cards and Christmas carols romanticize the birth of Jesus, which is not necessarily a bad thing, this was probably not what Mary would have envisioned for herself.

They arrive in Bethlehem to discover there is "no room for them in the inn," as many translations have it. It's doubtful that Bethlehem had a plethora of hotels waiting for weary travelers. More than likely, an inn would have referred to an empty room in either a stranger's or relative's home that could have been rented out or borrowed for times such as these. It would be more like today's bed-and-breakfasts in homes or Airbnbs, but probably without any hot croissants, coffee, and fresh orange juice waiting for guests when they wake up. In Jesus's day, on the first floor of homes, or immediately attached to them, would be a stable of sorts, consisting of a room where the owners' livestock would be brought in for the night. There was no room for Mary and Joseph in the inn, but the homeowner (or innkeeper) offered them the only space left in town: the barn.

No one dreams of having their baby in a stable, but ninety long miles from home, Mary and Joseph settle into their lowly accommodations, surrounded by the smell of farm animals. It's not that they would have been horrified by such conditions; after all, they would have had a similar layout at their own home. But they had probably never slept with animals before, let alone considered giving birth in the barn. It certainly wasn't perfect, but babies come on their own timing. Jesus certainly did.

I can imagine that at some point, Mary and Joseph might have been appreciative of the privacy the stable afforded them as Mary was delivering Jesus. They escaped the other visitors in the house hearing her laboring. They were alone. Alone, but not abandoned. They both knew that God was with them, just as God had been since the time of this precious child's conception. At his birth, they experienced what all parents do: the breaking in of joy in the midst of worry, concern, and even unwanted circumstances. They, no doubt, also did what all parents do: counted fingers and toes, and marveled at how beautiful their baby was. "Have you ever seen a more beautiful baby than him?" "No, never." They were overjoyed that God chose them to be parents to this special child. "And [she] wrapped him in bands of cloth and laid him in a manger."

We've all had Christmases where things didn't go as perfectly as planned. If you think about it, most Christmases don't go that way. The gifts you searched for high and low, at every toy store, and on every website, were unavailable. There was always one kid who wouldn't smile for the Christmas card. The corporate gift box under the tree contained chocolates that your dog ate, prompting a Christmas Eve rush to the doggie emergency room. The family member you had been looking forward to seeing all year discovered their flight got canceled just as they were about to board. You had a death in your family. It was the year your spouse decided to leave. And yet Christmas came anyway, and in the midst of it, even with the very unperfect edges, there were glimmers of joy, and the true meaning of Christmas came through.

We had one of those Christmases when our daughter was nine years old and our son was six. It seemed that nothing that season had been going right. I was in seminary, working at the church, and I hadn't yet had time to buy Christmas presents or send Christmas cards. *When,* I wondered, *am I going to have time to create the perfect Christmas for our children?* Haven't we all been there? To top it all off, I got a call one day from my daughter's school that I needed to come pick her up because she was sick. I brought her home, gave her medicine for her fever, put her to bed, and let her sleep. But when she awoke a couple of hours later, her fever had spiked, not gone down, and she was in a tremendous amount of pain. A visit to the pediatrician confirmed that Caroline had appendicitis, and it was feared her appendix had ruptured. All of a sudden, it didn't seem to matter that Christmas presents hadn't been bought or cards addressed; the only thing that mattered was this child. We drove straight from the doctor's office to the emergency room, where a surgeon and my husband would be waiting to meet us. Five days later, we were back at home, with few presents, but with a child who was well and alive.

The last week before Christmas was spent not in the chaos, hustle, and bustle of shopping, but at home, as a family. We spent our days quietly reading Christmas stories, watching Christmas movies, and wrapping the few gifts we had, together. We spent the time taking care of what was most important and unknowingly creating the most special Christmas memories of all. When our family talks about our most memorable or favorite Christmases, this one is usually the first one mentioned. It didn't resemble what we had envisioned as the perfect Christmas, but it ended up being just that.

The book *The Best Christmas Pageant Ever* provides poignant and comical examples of how this played out for an entire community who learns the meaning of Christmas, and what a perfect Christmas and the joy it brings looks like in reality.

In the book, the unruliest (and most unchurched) children in town, the Herdmans, weasel their way into the leading roles in the church's annual Christmas pageant. As a result, nothing goes as expected or planned. However, the awe of these children experiencing the birth of Jesus through eyes unclouded by familiarity, and their heartfelt improvisations of this ancient story, melt the hearts of the audience. During rehearsals, the Herdmans are furious that no one will make room for a pregnant woman at the inn. They also think the wise men's gifts are ridiculously unsuitable for a baby. And Imogene (Mary) is upset because Mary can't select her own baby's name.

On the night of the pageant, the Herdmans have a heart-tugging effect on all present. Imogene burps a doll version of baby Jesus before laying him in the manger. And the wise men, instead of laying gifts of gold, frankincense, and myrrh at the foot of Jesus's crib, reverently offer him the canned ham they have been given by the charitable works committee for their own Christmas dinner. Imogene cries as they all sing "Silent Night," giving the narrator the impression that she suddenly understands what Christmas is all about.

In the end, the Herdmans refuse to take the canned ham home with them, and everyone agrees that it was the best Christmas pageant ever, but no one knows exactly why. The narrator muses that it was because the Herdmans treated it as if it were a real event, not something they celebrated through an annual pageant, which helps her realize how little thought is normally put into it most years.

I stopped years ago being anxious about trying to make every Christmas a perfect one. I still buy presents, send Christmas cards (often late), and plan events for my family, but I also consciously don't let my expectations get too high, knowing that things will not always go as planned. Instead, these days, I try to keep my eyes and heart open for holy moments when they present themselves, unplanned (or in the case of the Herdmans, unscripted).

This past Christmas, small things happened that some people would have thought put a damper on the holiday, but they didn't. Not everyone made it to our home in Colorado by Christmas day, so we celebrated twice! There was so little snow this year, which made skiing (our family's favorite Christmastime activity) impossible. Instead, we worked on puzzles and played games indoors by the fire, offering more time for conversations with each family member—and what a precious gift that was. Baby Elizabeth cried all the way down the hill during her first sledding experience, but we all took it in stride (she wasn't crazy about seeing Santa for the first time either!). For several reasons, we weren't able to attend Christmas Eve services, which normally would have put me in a real funk. After all, I haven't missed a Christmas Eve service in more than thirty years. Nothing went quite as planned.

However, on Christmas Eve, after the Christmas story was read, I offered to give the baby her nighttime bottle and put her to bed. As I rocked her in the dimly lit room, I began to sing Christmas carols as lullabies to the unfathomably precious gift our family had been given this year. The carols that we would have sung at church that night were now softly surrounding our infant granddaughter: "O Come, All Ye Faithful," "Hark! The Herald Angels Sing," and "Angels We Have Heard on High," to name a few. But the night ended, as it would have at a candlelight service, with "Silent Night."

As I gently sang the words "Silent night, holy night, / All is calm, all is bright," I found that they described my own present reality, and I was overcome with awe at the Christmas story and God's continuing presence. I was cradling this child for whom we had all prayed and gave thanks for her precious life, and for the gift of the Christ Child, whom I prayed this child in my arms would come to know intimately. I also thought of Mary and Joseph and how their first Christmas probably did not begin as particularly calm or bright. But the day ended as a holy one, full of God's presence, and with the gift of new life—not just for them, but for all of us. It was the perfect Christmas.

Sometimes, our imperfect Christmases become perfect. And when that happens, we might also realize how little thought we put into them most years, or at least thought about what is most important to the season. That is what celebrating each week of Advent does for us liturgically. It focuses our attention on what is most important—on the words of the prophets, the longing of the people for a messiah, someone to save them, someone who can save all of us. Advent leads us to open our hearts to hope, joy, love, and peace. It opens our hearts to the surprise and joy of new opportunities, new calls from God. It opens our hearts to embracing new paths in our life. It stirs us to share our blessings out of the blessings and gifts that have been given to us, especially the gift of the Christ Child.

The Joy of New Neighbors and Sharing the Good News

Mary and Joseph's first Christmas was not spent as they had envisioned. I imagine their day began with equal amounts of worry, anxiety, broken dreams, fear, and darkness. But it ended in great joy that their son, God's Son, had been born to them. It also ended with the arrival of unexpected visitors who were overjoyed to meet a Savior that had been born *to them* on that very night:

> *When the angels had left them and gone into heaven, the shepherds said to one another, "Let us go now to Bethlehem and see this thing that has taken place, which the Lord has made known to us." So they went with haste and found Mary and Joseph and the child lying in the manger. When they saw this, they made known what had been told them about this child, and all who heard it were amazed at what the shepherds told them, and Mary treasured all these words and pondered them in her heart. The shepherds*

> *returned, glorifying and praising God for all they had heard and seen, just as it had been told them.*
>
> (*Luke 2:15-20*)

Mary and Joseph's plans for their wedding, and for the birth of their baby, had been broken. God and Caesar interrupted what they thought were their perfect plans. The shepherds' plans for a quiet evening tending sheep were also interrupted by God's messengers in a surprising, holy, and joy-filled manner. Their calm night was shattered by angel song and blazing light. Their ordinary watch became the first Christmas worship service. After the angels had left them, the shepherds were so overcome with joy and amazement at what the angels had said that they set out to find this Savior who had been born to and for them. They—*especially they*—were invited to go and meet this new born king.

The Christmas hymn "O Holy Night" contains these words: "Long lay the world in sin and error pining, / till He appeared and the soul felt its worth. / A thrill of hope, the weary world rejoices, / for yonder breaks a new and glorious morn!" On that glorious night, "the soul felt its worth." The shepherds, maybe for the first time in their lives, felt their true worth as God's beloved children and part of the building of God's kingdom.

So they run, as quickly as their feet can carry them, to Bethlehem to find their Messiah lying in a place that is all too familiar, and homelike, to them: a manger. King Jesus, this story tells us, is far more comfortable in these humble surroundings than in the marbled, golden halls of power. We see this further illustrated in his life as he calls fishermen to be his disciples; invites sinners, prostitutes, and tax collectors to dine with him; feeds the hungry; heals the sick; and calls women to be the first to share the news of his resurrection. Shepherds announced his birth, and women announced his resurrection—good news so great that it begged immediate heralding.

Have you ever been the recipient of great news that brought such joy that you could not wait to share it? What about when you were accepted to your college of choice or were offered a job you longed for? What about when you became engaged or found out you were going to have a baby? I don't know about you, but I couldn't wait to share the incredible news with anyone who would listen! This is how it must have felt, but on a grander scale, to be one of these shepherds.

My guess is that it wasn't too difficult to find the one baby who had been born in a stable in Bethlehem that night. The shepherds arrive breathless at the humble dwelling, where the Messiah lay sleeping. While Mary and Joseph have been counting baby fingers and toes, and marveling at their new, perfect son, the shepherds have had an encounter with the divine that must be shared! It seems they couldn't wait to proclaim *everything* the angels had told them about Jesus. Not only that, it seems that they told not only Mary and Joseph but anyone and everyone else who would listen, for the scripture tells us that "all who heard [this news] were amazed at what the shepherds told them" (Luke 2:18).

Good news is hard to hold on to. It has to be shared. What a blessing it must have been for Mary and Joseph to hear confirmation from the shepherds of what God had revealed to them many months before. Now they had others to share their joy with—people who had, within minutes, become welcome neighbors and friends.

While we know that the Nativity wasn't as Christmas card artists portray, and that we don't need to romanticize the reality of what Mary and Joseph experienced during their first Christmas, those images for us are theologically captivating ones that capture our hearts and imaginations: Mary, Joseph, and the shepherds, with their faces illuminated by soft lantern light, lovingly surrounding a straw-filled manger, as a gentle cow and lamb quietly observe the scene. And at the center of that scene is the precious Christ Child. The significance of these images is that they represent to us a sense of home—a new home, and a new family, whose center is a child, a Savior born to us all. He is the center of Mary and Joseph's life, of the angels' announcement, and of the shepherds' newest calling (to share the good news of Christ's birth). Wherever the Christ is present, these images portray, is home. He created a home with Mary and Joseph in their acceptance of God's call on their lives. He created a home among strangers-become-neighbors in the wise men and shepherds through their visits to the Holy Family. He brought me back home on a mountaintop with strangers become neighbors in service to one who was in need of care, and in the cradling of my granddaughter on the holy night of the Christ Child's birth. He is the one who leads you home in the midst of your broken plans and life detours. He is Emmanuel, "God with us," no matter where we might be or in what circumstances we find ourselves. He is born to us, in us, and for us to bring good news of great joy and peace, to all people. In return for this great gift given to us, we, like the shepherds, are to answer a new call to share that great gift with others, proclaiming God's good news of great joy through word and action.

During this Advent and Christmas season, may you experience, even in the midst of broken plans, God's surprises and great joy and peace. The kind of joy and peace that comes from people, communities, and neighbors extending God's love beyond the walls of their homes and even churches to extend into the world in all directions. And no matter where you go this season and beyond, may you, like the angels and shepherds, break through others' darkness and carry good news of great joy to those who are waiting with hope to hear it.

ACKNOWLEDGMENTS

It is always my hope as a minister and a writer that my words, whether they be spoken or written, will lead others to experience more fully the incomprehensible depth of God's love and grace through Jesus the Christ. And so, I am most grateful to you, the readers, who have purposefully committed your time to join me on this journey to seek God's surprises for you during this Advent season. I pray that these words have drawn you closer to the One who was born, and continues to be born, to you each day, and that they will be an inspiration to you in your journey toward Christmas and in service to your neighbors throughout the year.

Bringing a book to life seems as if it should be a simple prospect. Writing, however, is only the beginning of the publishing process. Numerous others' fingerprints are all over these pages.

I am grateful to Maria Mayo for inviting me to write this book and am indebted to you for your confidence in placing this study (and so many others) in my hands and for the brainstorming sessions that led to the birth of this book.

An enormous debt of gratitude goes to my editor, James Rogers, for smoothing out clunky sentences, rightfully questioning some theological statements, delicately suggesting that some material be shortened or removed for your, the reader's, benefit, and for quietly correcting my love of commas. Thank you, James, for your skillful expertise in both editing and theology.

A host of others on the Abingdon team were also invaluable in the production and publication of this book. To Trenton Waterson, for hours spent setting up filming locations, making sure every scene looked just right, and for ensuring that travel arrangements to Nashville were seamless; to Tim Cobb for your meticulous work in laying out the book and following it step-by-step through production; to Catey Miller for using your wonderful writing skills in tying the leader guide to the text and videos; and to all at Abingdon Press who have made this book and study a reality, "thank you" hardly seems adequate, but my gratitude for you is enormous.

To the Highland Park UMC Women's Bible Study, I am beyond blessed and grateful that you continue to allow me to teach material for my books to you prior to their publication. Your insights and the sharing of your questions and personal stories always bring clarity and offer shape to the written pages of my books, especially this one. Your contributions are appreciated more than you can ever know. Much love to you all.

Finally, to my husband, Ike, your coming into my life was God's greatest surprise and joy by far. We have, with God's help, navigated many broken paths and always found through them God's blessings. I am grateful to you for your endless support and patience as I answer God's call to write, and I am grateful to God for you and the life we are blessed to share.

NOTES

Preface

1 Charles Wesley (lyrics, 1744), "Come, Thou Long Expected Jesus," *The United Methodist Hymnal* (The United Methodist Publishing House, 1989), #196.

Chapter 1

1 Ashley Cleere Cook, "Luke 1:26-38," in *Feasting on the Word: Preaching the Revised Common Lectionary*, ed. David L. Bartlett and Barbara Brown Taylor (Westminster John Knox Press, 2008), 96.

2 John Wesley, *Explanatory Notes upon the New Testament* (Baker, 1983), Luke 1:46.

3 For the inspiration for this section and the importance of "has" here, see "Diana Butler Bass, Author of 'A Beautiful Year'—Richard Rohr's 'Daily Meditations,'" Center for Action and Contemplation, interview of Bass by Mark Longhurst, posted February 9, 2026, https://www.youtube.com/watch?v=NDMV8AIdJtI.

Chapter 2

1 Adapted from Raymond E. Brown, *The Birth of the Messiah: A Commentary on the Infancy Narratives in the Gospels of Matthew and Luke* (Doubleday, 1993), 34–35.

Chapter 3

1 John H. Hopkins (lyrics, 1857), "We Three Kings of Orient Are," *The United Methodist Hymnal* (The United Methodist Publishing House, 1989), #254.

2 Henry Wadsworth Longfellow, "The Three Kings," The Poetry Foundation, https://www.poetryfoundation.org/poems/57830/the-three-kings.
3 Thomas G. Long, *Matthew* (Westminster John Knox Press, 1997), 18.
4 "Congregational Reaffirmation of the Baptismal Covenant," *The United Methodist Book of Worship* (United Methodist Publishing House, 1992).

Chapter 4

1 Band Together Texas, "Texas Flood Hero: Camp Counselor Saves 16 Girls," produced by Craig Parks, posted August 27, 2025, by Miranda Lambert, https://youtu.be/fUxsXStADUc; Emmaneul Acho, "Tragedy at Camp Mystic: 27 Lives Lost, but Their Faith Lives On," posted August 6, 2025, by Emmaneul Acho, https://youtu.be/1_0XfxaiiGY.